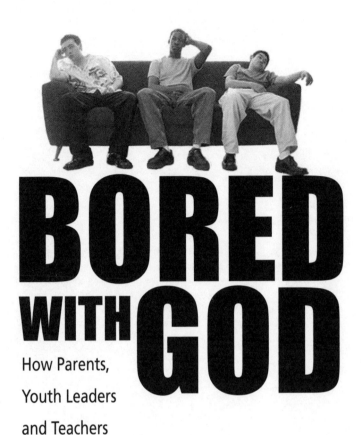

BORED
WITH GOD

How Parents,
Youth Leaders
and Teachers
Can Overcome
Student Apathy

SEAN DUNN

ivp

InterVarsity Press
Downers Grove, Illinois

InterVarsity Press
P.O. Box 1400, Downers Grove, IL 60515-1426
World Wide Web: www.ivpress.com
E-mail: mail@ivpress.com

InterVarsity Press® is the book-publishing division of InterVarsity Christian Fellowship/USA®, a student movement active on campus at hundreds of universities, colleges and schools of nursing in the United States of America, and a member movement of the International Fellowship of Evangelical Students. For information about local and regional activities, write Public Relations Dept., InterVarsity Christian Fellowship/USA, 6400 Schroeder Rd., P.O. Box 7895, Madison, WI 53707-7895, or visit the IVCF website at <www.intervarsity.org>.

All Scripture quotations, unless otherwise indicated, are taken from the Holy Bible, New International Version®. NIV®. Copyright ©1973, 1978, 1984 by International Bible Society. Used by permission of Zondervan Publishing House. All rights reserved.

Design: Cindy Kiple

Images: red couch: Ryan McVay/Getty Images
three guys: ImageState

ISBN 0-8308-3206-8

Printed in the United States of America ∞

Library of Congress Cataloging-in-Publication Data

Dunn, Sean, 1968-
  Bored with God: how parents, youth leaders, and teachers can
overcome student apathy / Sean Dunn.
     p. c.m.
Includes bibliographical references.
ISBN 0-8308-3206-8 (pbk.: alk. paper)
1. Church work with youth. 2. Christian youth—Religious life. 3.
Church work with youth. 4. Students—Religious life. I. Title.
  BV4447.D87 2004
   259'.23—dc22

                                                                2003027936

P	19	18	17	16	15	14	13	12	11	10	9	8	7	6	5	4	3	2	1
Y	19	18	17	16	15	14	13	12	11	10	09	08	07	06	05	04				

To my short, beautiful and blonde wife, Mary.

It is your selflessness, servanthood and willingness

to sacrifice that allows us to contend for a generation.

You are everything that I ever wanted and

needed in a partner and friend.

I love you with my whole heart.

CONTENTS

A SPIRITUAL HABIT
OR A HOLY PASSION?

They are surrounded by the most exciting opportunity that anyone could ever know, and yet many of them take it for granted. Young people who grow up in church sit through countless biblical teachings and attend all sorts of church camps and conferences. They sing dangerous songs about knowing God personally, drawing near to his heart and being used as his hands and feet. Yet many of them sing as though this were a spiritual hobby instead of a holy passion.

Consider Beth and Bryce, siblings whose approaches to God were vastly different. Beth was on fire for God. Her zeal was evident in our youth meetings and at our events. She wanted to know God intimately and personally, and she realized that the time she spent investing in her spiritual life was not a duty but an opportunity.

Bryce, on the other hand, was moral but apathetic. He was faithful in attendance but not aggressive in his personal pursuit of God. He did not see the value in studying the Bible, praying to God or building a healthy quiet time.

Beth and Bryce heard the same messages, attended the same camps, sang the same songs and were raised the same way. Both were good kids, but one had a strong and growing faith, while the other had a stagnant faith. One was bold with her beliefs, while the other was intimidated to share with others what he knew to be true. One was building a love relationship with her Creator, while the other was lay-ing the groundwork for a frustrated faith and a fruitless spiritual life.

Many years have passed since Beth and Bryce were in my care, but the patterns they established back then set the course for their spiritual journeys. In many ways those patterns have contributed to who they are even now as adults. Beth is active in church, walking with God. Although Bryce considers himself a Christian, he no longer attends church, and his faith is something that he never thinks about. Apathy still dominates his life.

In more than fifteen years of youth ministry I have worked with, observed and cared for thousands of students. Although their stories vary, they typically resemble either Bryce or Beth in the ways that they approach God. Their spiritual life can be defined either by the hunger that drives them into God's presence on a regular basis or by apathy that inspires neglect. Every area of their life will be affected by Christ if they thirst for him and spend time with him. But if apathy has grabbed hold of their life, then their spiritual progress will be limited at best.

Within the pages of this book you will discover tools for igniting a passion for Christ in your students. As you read, you will uncover apathy's games and boredom's effects. You will learn how to discern and effectively address the problems youth have in their spiritual life. You will discover helps but also hope. You will be inspired in your own relationship with Christ even as you become focused for the task of leading the students in your life.

God will not confront our students' apathy without helping them change, and we may be God's hands and feet in the process of their transformation. With God's help, we will see our youth transformed from bored students to aggressive, on-fire Christians with a deep connection to their Father and an effective approach to life.

1

THEY KNOW IT ALL, BUT . . .

A young pastor was about to go up on the platform to perform his duties for the weekend service when an usher approached him to talk. In whispered tones, the usher told his pastor that his zipper was down. The pastor thanked the usher profusely. "Well, I love you too much to let you go out there and embarrass yourself," the usher responded.

The pastor's problem would probably have gone unnoticed at first, but if it hadn't been rectified, eventually it would have brought him embarrassment. Something similar is happening in the Christian culture. Many students are going out into the world with a defining problem that will cause not only embarrassment but ineffectiveness, frustration and frail faith. The symptoms (weak convictions, limited power, dominating sins and limited spiritual fruit) are being acknowledged and addressed by religious leaders and institutions, but the cause of the problem is often ignored. Spiritual apathy is derailing the religious commitment of many of our students, and it is a topic that we must address.

SPIRITUAL APATHY: A PLAY IN FIVE ACTS

The curtain is about to go up; act one is about to begin.

She quickly checks her wardrobe to make sure that she "represents" properly. Her Christian T-shirt is proclaiming her faith, and her bracelet is spouting a message in code. Her lines are memorized, and her smile is in place. She purposefully steps out of her car, grabs the Bible out of her back seat and heads into the youth room.

Act one. She walks through the room, making sure to say hello to all of the "pretty" people while avoiding those who are unattractive or unpopular or whose reputations are less than perfect. The hugs she distributes are all part of the routine that she has worked up, as is the little laugh she flaunts to try to impress the people around her. All the while she is judgmentally picking apart everyone and everything she sees.

Act two. The service starts, and she finds her seat in the front of the room. When the music begins she jumps right in. She claps, sings, does the corresponding hand motions and appropriately closes her eyes to represent a prayerful attitude. Meanwhile, her mind is spinning, jumping from one thought to another. For a moment she dwells on a girl she doesn't like, who is sitting across the room. Then she thinks about the guy sitting next to her, whom she does like. She wonders if the youth leader is looking at her in her reflective state. *I hope he's impressed,* she thinks.

Act three. The youth leader gives a talk on forgiveness, and she follows in her Bible, smiling and nodding at just the right times. She dresses up her performance in gestures and phrases and hopes that she's convincing in her role as an attentive listener.

Act four. After the service, she joins some of the youth leaders and students at the restaurant down the street. She hears some of the younger kids saying mean things about someone, and she quickly runs in to stop the gossip and quotes a spiritual proverb at them. After that she finds the youth pastor to tell him that she was "very moved" by his message.

Act five. She walks into her room and puts her Bible back on its shelf, where it will sit until church next Sunday. Turning on her television, she flips to a show and starts to snicker and blush as the characters practice backbiting and make innuendoes. Before her head hits her pillow, she glances over at the picture of her boyfriend sitting next to her bed. For the first time this evening, her smile fades as she thinks, *I hope no one figures out what we are doing. I would die if they did.* Without praying she goes to sleep.

She needs her rest; tomorrow she has another show to put on.

FROM SPIRITUAL APATHY TO TRUE HUNGER

Much to God's dismay we are raising a generation of young people who know a great deal about him but who don't really know him. They can recite Scripture and look impressive, but if they continue to keep God at a distance, they will grow up to be

- weak
- timid
- petty
- self-righteous
- antagonistic
- frustrated
- self-obsessed
- arrogant
- uninterested
- undisciplined
- unreliable
- unpredictable
- unstable

Christians all over the globe are tormented by apathy. This silent influencer keeps them from running after the One who is desperate to walk in relationship with them. Apathy dulls the spiritual senses and whispers lies of security to those who are infected. It is the door through which sin enters and faith leaves.

Without desire for God, the young people we care about are doomed to live complacent and pathetic Christian lives. With God's help, parents, teachers and Christian leaders can move students toward a hunger for him. We can stir their passions and remind them of their first love. A true hunger for God helps students become

- passionate
- pursuers of Christ
- solid in their convictions
- bold
- stable
- faithful
- motivated
- teachable
- moved by a heart for God and the world
- eager to serve society and God's kingdom

LEADING STUDENTS TO LIVING WATER

A young person's faith will be stable only as he or she learns who God is and falls in love with him. While no human being can create experiences with God that lead students into such a relationship, there are some things that can be done to encourage them in that general direction.

Our first step should be to pray for discernment and to confront the masks that students wear. It is imperative that we see through such façades to what's really going on inside them. When we recognize that students are playing games with us, we must lovingly confront them. We must care too much to look the other way. By affirming and convincing students of our commitment to them, we move them away from shallow tendencies and toward an authentic expression of their faith.

We must teach also our students to point their eyes heavenward. As humans we have a desire to be needed. Although students need guidance from good leaders, we often take on too much of the responsibility for their knowledge about God. We want them to blindly adopt our opinions rather than work out their own understanding. Instead, we must help young people learn how to think for themselves with God's perspective as their foundation and the Word of God as their rule. God declares in Scripture that as Christians

We must help our students see God in the fullness of who he is.

we can know God's will (see Acts 22:14; Romans 12:2). He wants us to look to him for guidance. Convincing our students that God really is waiting to whisper his plans and desires directly into their hearts is difficult, but it is necessary.

We can teach our students to see God and fall in love with him. It is possible to create attractive pictures of God's goodness, grace and love. We must help them see his desire and passion for them. We have to show them that they can experience his presence and comfort and know his might and power. If they see God in the fullness of who he is, they will be captivated.

STEVE'S STORY

Steve was looking forward to his first year at Bible college, because he assumed that the Christian community, the Bible classes and the spiritual climate of the campus would help accelerate his spiritual growth and bring him closer to Christ.

However, Steve's assumptions were wrong. His college experience did not naturally draw him closer to God; instead, apathy crept in. Late nights and early mornings stole the time that Steve had once given to God. After a few months Steve was spiritually dry, unable to really pray and too undisciplined to push past the barrier that stood in his way.

Then Steve met Rob. They met on the basketball court where they began to hold marathon one-on-one matches. Eventually their friendship evolved into something beyond sports and took a spiritual turn. Because Rob was older and more spiritually mature, he had identified Steve as someone he could invest in. Rob began to invite Steve to his prayer times. Several times a week, early in the morning, Rob would pick up Steve at his dorm and the two of them would sit in Rob's car praying together with a worship tape playing in the background.

Although Steve did not realize what was happening, he was seeing in Rob someone who enjoyed feasting at God's table. Rob loved God and actively pursued his presence. Rather than merely hearing about this type of hunger, Steve was getting to participate in it. He saw a man whose heart was tender, who loved worship and who longed to be close to God. For Rob, it was more than a discipline; spending time with God was an opportunity to be braided together in intimacy with Christ.

Silently, an impartation was taking place. Steve was picking up some of Rob's attributes. He was becoming more tender before God. He was beginning to lose himself in worship, and he started looking forward to time spent in prayer.

Steve's first year in college proved to be a remarkable and exciting year of growth. He doesn't credit it to the classes, chapels or community. He doesn't attribute it to his pastor, professors or roommates. If you ask him, he will say that he began to grow significantly when a more mature Christian targeted him and intentionally modeled spiritual hunger for him.

When Steve returned for his second year, Rob did not. But that didn't slow down Steve's pursuit of God. Because of Rob's encouragement, challenge and model, Steve had developed a habit of meeting with God and embraced a lifestyle of intimacy with his Creator. What he saw in Rob got him started, but the pleasure that he discovered in God's presence has helped him continue to flourish.

THE ULTIMATE GOAL

The ultimate goal in every home and youth ministry should be to draw young people to a place where they are walking intimately with God. Rather than living their faith through parents and leaders, it is imperative that they develop a spiritual hunger that keeps them running after God even when no one else is around. If they have hunger, they will grow. Without it, they will simply exist.

2

FROM SELF-RIGHTEOUSNESS TO HUMILITY

I was approached after a youth service by three young men who had grown up in the church. They had something they wanted to discuss with me, and they invited me to go with them to a burger place to talk. As I drove to the restaurant, I had a feeling that we were about to have a very shallow conversation. I wasn't wrong.

One of the students, Rick, began by telling me that he and his friends did not like the fact that our youth ministry was attracting young people with "reputations" and "addictions." They were especially bothered by the teens who were driving into the church parking lot with cigarettes lit up.

After Rick said his piece, I thought for a minute and then responded in this way: "You know, Rick, I like the fact that we have smokers coming to our youth ministry. I am proud that our church has the ability to accept people who aren't perfect. As a matter of fact, I am committed to getting those people to our youth meetings for two reasons. First of all, they need God. If we convinced them that they had to be perfect to come to our church, then they would waste their Wednesday nights at McDonalds instead of coming to youth group to hear about the God who loves them and desperately wants to be a part of their lives. The second reason is that if we didn't have people who are living far from God's will for their lives, we might produce nothing more than a bunch of self-righteous Christian kids with no heart for the world."

Our conversation ended at that point because Rick did not like my response. I don't think he ever came back to our youth meetings after that conversation.

SUPERIORITY UNMASKED

In my yearly travels to hundreds of churches I become more and more aware that our youth groups are full of self-righteous young people. Many times the trend can be attributed to apathy. When students become stagnant in their spiritual journey and their pursuit of the Creator slows, they lose connection with the One who can change them from the inside out. The natural effect is that they begin to neglect their internal issues as they concentrate on their external performances, resulting in an arrogance that convinces them that they are doing relatively well compared to others. It is then that the spiritual erosion begins. The students' faith suffers, as does their witness to others. While individuals always vary in characteristics and behavior, there are some traits that are common among self-righteous students.

Resistance to change. These students oppose change because they are convinced that every opinion they have is from God. In order to protect what they "know" is right, they will fight against the direction and vision that God has given to parents and leaders who have authority over them.

Julie, for example, had always been a challenging child to raise. She was strong-willed, and she had perfected the art of emotional manipulation in order to get her way. She felt that her opinions were right and other ideas didn't merit her attention.

When she was fifteen, Julie's father told his family that the Lord was leading them to move to a different church. Julie was quick to argue that going to a new church was a mistake. She pointed out how ungodly the teens in the new church were, and when that didn't work, she was defiant and said she wouldn't go.

Julie's dad stood his ground and made her go to the new church. For the first month she argued and whined, but after a few weeks she gave up. She realized that her fight was in vain, and she decided that the new church wasn't so bad after all.

Submitting to God and his direction and will are foundational to a Christian's faith. As we submit to him, we will be confronted with opportunities to change as he leads. When we do that, growth occurs. When apathy sneaks in, however, it teaches that any path that is unfamiliar or uncomfortable is unnecessary. That is when spiritual growth stops.

Unrealistic self-images. Self-righteous students often can't see clear images of themselves and struggle to identify areas in their own life that they need to work on. When a spiritual leader or parent tries to highlight a problem area, self-righteous students typically ignore or argue against the correction. They refuse to see themselves in the light of reality, because they find it easier to point out the faults of others instead.

This is a dangerous place in which to be. Students who think they're "doing okay" won't recognize their need to be close to Christ and to become more like him. As a result, spiritual growth for these students is limited.

Lack of spiritual fruit. Since self-righteous youth tend to lack compassion and think only about themselves, there is no spiritual multiplication as a result of their contact with others. Selfishness rules in their hearts, and things that don't affect them directly are of no importance to them. They believe that since they have made their decisions to be Christians, obeying Jesus' command to practice evangelism isn't enough to make associating with the world worth their while (unless, of course, the "evangelism" benefits them in some way, such as giving them the opportunity to impress others or meet an attractive boy or girl).

In addition, these young people have an incredible ability to use their negativity to create an exclusive bubble that insulates them from the peers they deem imperfect. Their critical spirits make them hard to be around (Proverbs 13:10 teaches that pride breeds quarrels), and eventually people will begin to avoid the places where they hang out. That is why many church youth groups struggle to keep new students after the first visit.

OVERCOMING SELF-RIGHTEOUSNESS

John Ruskin made a statement that is very profound: "When a man is wrapped up in himself, he makes a pretty small package." When our students are self-absorbed and self-righteous, they are tiny indeed. Unfortunately, "small" people can often create big disturbances.

As an individual who has been given responsibility for the spiritual development of students, you cannot ignore the self-righteous attitude that is prevalent among many of our youth. This attitude is difficult to detect and deal with, because it braids itself together with the very fibers of a person's being. With God's help you must engage in the spiritual warfare necessary to influence your students in the fight against self-righteousness.

Prayer. Because self-righteousness is so hard to deal with, prayer must lay the groundwork. Pray that the Spirit of God will convict students of their wrong attitudes. Pray that they will be broken before God and recognize their own depravity. The words in Matthew 9:36 can be adapted into this prayer: "God, allow my son to see the world the way that you do. May he be moved by compassion when he sees people who are harassed, helpless and leaderless. May something inside of him want to respond to their needs instead of adding to their alienation."

You can also lead students in praying about this issue themselves. Suggest that they pray Psalm 139:23-24, "Show me if there is any offensive way in me." If students willingly pray this prayer, in time God will highlight their weaknesses and begin to bring about change in their lives.

Humility. As you seek to defeat the self-righteousness that silently attacks your students, you must not just pray but also model humility for them. When humility is authentic and sincere, it is contagious.

Through Scripture, God confronts ungodly attitudes and cultivates proper characteristics.

When people see someone who lives a surrendered life, who honestly puts others first and is not caught up in making a name for him or herself, they will take notice. If you practice humility, those closest to you will recognize your humble spirit, and they will embrace that attitude as well.

The problem is that even church leaders have been known to model self-righteousness, and parents have often refused to admit their own failures. By hiding behind their own masks and refusing to walk in authentic humility, they have unknowingly trained others in the trade of self-righteousness. If the trend is going to change in our families and churches, it must begin with us.

One of the best ways to model humility is to be quick to ask forgiveness and admit when we are wrong. When we humble ourselves to that vulnerable place, we are making a statement that being real is more important than being right.

Responsibility. Let your students know that they are responsible for fighting off self-righteousness and its side effects (such as bitterness, selfishness and pride) before these characteristics can take root in their heart.

One way to go about this is to positively reinforce proper attitudes when you see them. For example, you might say, "Tom, I just wanted to thank you for helping clean up after our activity the other night. I have really been impressed with your servant's heart." Or you might say, "You know, Jill, because everyone looks up to you so much, it would be so easy for you to let pride creep in. I appreciate the fact that you are so humble and real. That is a testimony to your relationship with Christ."

Another way to help students fend off self-righteousness is to point to the biblical stories of people whose destinies were affected by pride (King Belshazzar in Daniel 5) and those who effectively avoided it (Paul and Barnabas in Acts 14). Through these stories you can share with students the dangers of letting self-righteousness infiltrate their lives and demonstrate that dealing with pride is an ongoing battle, one that must not be ignored.

Tough love. If it is obvious that your students deal with self-righteousness, then you have a responsibility to protect them from circumstances that will add to the problem. You might consider removing them from responsibilities at church for which they will be given excessive praise if you believe that they are performing their duties without any true sincerity.

For example, several years ago there was a young lady who began traveling with our ministry. She was very talented, so naturally we put her to work. We didn't question her character, because she came with solid references and the appearance of a servant's heart. However, we soon realized that she was more show than substance. She felt superior to everyone on our team, and it came out in critical re marks and condescending tones. Out of a desire to protect the people we traveled with and ministered to, and in the hope of seeing her develop the inner character that would allow her to be effective for God, we took her off the stage and out of leadership and began to talk about these heart issues.

As you can imagine, she didn't like that. She pointed out her superiority over the people who were doing the jobs that she wanted and used our prayer meetings to illuminate what she felt was our mistake. When we held fast to our decision she left our team and went to a place where she could get more stage time. Ever since, she's been jumping from place to place, seeking the spotlight but ignoring the conviction of the Holy Spirit.

The fruit of a critical spirit will be evident in every church and work situation self-righteous people will ever have, and they will not be productive for the kingdom of God. I don't like taking the hard line with these students, but sometimes it is the only thing that will get through to them. And, in another vein, I am not only trying to prepare that individual for future success; I am also shielding others so that they don't see that destructive behavior modeled and rewarded.

WITNESSES TO THE WORLD

With God's help we can see even the most difficult students turn from their self-righteousness. After our conversation, Eric and Jeremy (Rick's friends from the story I told at the beginning of this chapter) returned to our youth ministry with changed attitudes. They checked their "holier-than-thou" attitudes at the door and came in with an understanding that they had an opportunity to be blessings to those they had previously avoided. Instead of huddling in their own little group, they began to wander around the room looking for people to engage in conversation. When it came time for the message, they didn't sit in the seats that they had occupied for years; they moved back a few rows and sat with students from the alternative high school.

From that moment on, Eric and Jeremy became leaders in our group and evangelists in their schools. They had hearts of compassion and an understanding that God's kingdom demands that they reach out to others. Although losing Rick from our youth group was disappointing, I was grateful for the two who had stepped out of their self-righteousness and into maturity. And I was thankful for the way they influenced others through their witness.

About a year after they graduated, I received a letter from Jeremy, who took some time to thank me for the investment that I had made in his life. One of the lines from that letter still sticks in my memory: "Thanks for challenging me to be all that God wanted me to be and for helping me see the world the way that God sees it."

It is up to us to become God's willing instruments in teaching our students about the dangers of self-righteousness. After all, they are the next generation of witnesses to the world.

3

SHAKING UP THE FAMILIAR

As they entered the room, they had defiance written all over their faces. They took their seats in the back row and assumed "the pose." Their posture and their facial expressions made it clear that they were not excited about being in yet another chapel service.

Although this does not describe all of the students in the room that day, it definitely paints an accurate picture of the majority of them. Instead of well-equipped students who were focused on being positive influences on the world, this school was filled with bored and apathetic people who did not take their faith seriously. Chapels were dreaded by many of the students, who did not look forward to being challenged by the biblical principles they were working overtime to ignore. Their small Christian school had been infected with a disease, and they had been affected by its subtle yet dangerous pull.

The problem was that the students had become so familiar with their faith that they took it for granted. They had so many assumptions about church, Christianity and who God is that they regularly missed the real presence of God and the evidence of his hand at work all around them.

FAMILIARITY AT WORK

One of my spiritual mentors recently made a statement that applies here: "Familiarity steals greatness." Although we should become more and more amazed at Christ the more that we learn about him, the opposite often occurs. Instead of falling more in love with him, becoming more astonished by who he is and what he has done and more aware of the awesome opportunity that we have to grow closer to him, many of us take him for granted. We allow boredom to creep into our faith journeys and begin to take the abundant life he promised for granted.

Many young people are moral, outspoken about their faith and regular church attenders, yet all of these things often fade away unless the way that they approach God changes. When familiarity turns passionate Christians into apathetic ones, danger is crouching at the door. The characteristics that define the journeys of apathetic Christians are damaging to them as well as dangerous to those around them.

Arrogance and disrespect. Students who have become too familiar with God are convinced that their knowledge of spiritual things and their church heritage have positioned them well above others. They are defiant, argumentative and aggressive. They don't respect authority because they believe that they are above it.

I saw this at work while I was a student at a Christian college. Students who should have known that there is blessing in submitting to authority pushed the boundaries and created tension between themselves and the school's administration. Even their playful pranks were laced with opposition and challenge. Take, for example, the men's dorm residents who made it a point to break every rule in the student handbook in their yearbook picture. They wore T-shirts with alcohol advertisements on them, held "illegal" appliances and stolen campus road signs in their hands, had cigars in their mouths and snuck girls up to their hall for the photo. Although these infractions were all committed in a "tongue-in-cheek" manner, there was a statement included in their actions: "You have no authority over me!"

These students were upperclassmen, and most of them were leaders among their peers, but a few years of familiarity with the school's administration had made them lose respect. In turn, they didn't think twice about challenging authority. They not only broke the rules regularly, they also flaunted their lack of submission and influenced others in that direction as well. When the administration of the college refused to allow the picture to go into the yearbook, the students didn't respect that decision either. They made and handed out hundreds of autographed copies of the photo on campus.

Although students like this claim to be surrendered to God, their obedience to him is selective. They are aware of what the Bible says about submission to parents and to authority, yet they ignore or argue with those placed above them anyway.

Double standards. Typically, these students are marked by their hypocrisy. They can answer questions and win debates, but they don't take what they know and apply it to their own lives. They are the first ones to point out how others are falling short of God's mandates, but they don't recognize their own weak areas.

Because their familiarity has stolen their awe of God, they critically evaluate others' lives while accepting a more lenient approach to their own. When it comes to personal issues, they will take God's commands lightly. They are comfortable in their sin as long as it is not exposed or considered "shocking" in Christian circles. They are content knowing and proclaiming what is right even if their lives don't measure up.

FIXING FAMILIARITY

In a parenting group, one mother offered hope to others who might be in a frustrating place with their teens. Her testimony began with a son in his midteens who had grown up in the church and knew all of the answers (he actually had done well as a Bible quizzer for two years) but lived selfishly, not applying any of the truths that he could so confidently articulate. The woman told the group that at one point his behavior drove her to her wit's end. It was at that point that she could do nothing else other than commit her child to the Lord and ask him to do a work in her son's life.

It was less than a year later when her son went away to a Christian convention (solely for social reasons), met God in a personal way and came home a different person. Instead of studying the Scriptures in order to get the answers right, he began to read his Bible with interest. His critical spirit began to soften, and his mother noticed that he was beginning to pray for the people in his life. Instead of smirking at those who lived obviously sinful lifestyles, he was noticeably burdened for them and would go out of his way to engage them in conversation.

With a faith that only comes from personally watching a miracle occur, the woman told the other parents, "Don't give up. I know that it may look hopeless, but God will come through. He loves your son or daughter more than you do, and he will not let them run forever."

Ask God to remove their familiarity and replace it with a newfound awe of him.

Be in prayer. Prayer is the tool that softens the hardest hearts and warms the coldest spirits. It looses the shackles that bind those who are oppressed—and these students are very bound. If we want to see our students start to grow past their familiarity and into genuine relationships with God, we will start by praying. We must pray aggressively—and often. We must ask God to intervene, for we know that without his help, nothing positive will be accomplished. Make this topic a main point on your prayer list.

One prayer you can use as a guide is this adaptation of Paul's prayer from Ephesians 1:16-19: "Lord, I thank you for Tracy. God, I ask you to give her the Spirit of wisdom and revelation so that she may know you better. I pray also that the eyes of her heart will be enlightened so that she may know the hope to which you have called her, the riches that are hers and the incomparably great power that is available to her." In prayer, give your student to the Lord and rest in the fact that God is able to keep that which you entrust to him (2 Timothy 1:12).

Be direct. In your interactions with students your approach must be direct. Students who have been infected with boredom do not respond to fluff or shallow conversation. As you start to get a read on them (don't forget to ask God to give you incredible wisdom), openly and aggressively share with them what you are sensing. They may respond, and they may not (this is a spiritual battle, so there are no direct formulas or immediate fixes), but their response to your directness will be much better than if you had danced around the real issue.

When talking with one student, Peter, I sensed that the spiritual smile he was wearing was a front. Socially he was doing well, but my gut was telling me that he was spiritually dry. When I asked him how his spiritual life was going, he quickly answered, "Great!" but I sensed that he was not being entirely honest because he assumed I was expecting something better than he could offer. "Really?" I asked as I looked at him with concern. When he realized that I already knew he was struggling, he opened up to me, and together we were able to work toward revitalizing his faith. By being forthright, I let Peter know that I was aware of his struggle and that I was serious about talking about it. If I had been less direct in my approach, he may never have been fully honest with me.

Be gentle. Your students will respond better if you speak directly, with confidence and conviction. However, the strength that you show must be accompanied by noticeable care in your tone, your posture and your facial expression. Work hard to soften hard features that might communicate disappointment and to soften tones that come out harshly. Make it a point to speak softly. Quieter tones always convey kindness and care. Gentleness, paired with directness, will make your students comfortable enough with you to discuss the real issues in their lives.

If you want to push them toward God, you need to highlight their need for him.

Be focused—and patient. Students who have become too familiar with God tend to avoid discussing important topics, such as their personal devotional life and what God expects of them. Instead of having a revealing and honest conversation about what is lacking in their spiritual life, they would rather debate external issues (hypocrisy in the church, for example). Don't get tricked into debating things that really don't matter. If you want to push students toward God, then you need to focus on their spiritual life and their need for God (see Psalm 107:9; Matthew 5:6; 6:33).

After one youth service, a student named Lisa came to me and wanted to talk about some comments I had made about a musician she respected greatly. She felt that my opinions about the musician were judgmental. I told her that I did not have any bad feelings toward the musician, but that I was praying that he would encounter Christ and realize that he had a greater purpose in life than just to make music and become famous. Realizing that I had not satisfied Lisa's frustration, I sincerely asked her to forgive me for any wrong attitude I may have had. Then I tried to turn the conversation back to her. "Lisa, how are you doing with Christ?" She would have none of it. She still wanted to talk about the musician. As much as I tried to engage her in a personal spiritual discussion, she refused. Somewhat frustrated, but recognizing that there is a time and a season for everything, I ended the conversation.

As Lisa walked away, I prayed that God would bring her to a place where she would be able to address her own journey of faith. Although I would love to complete every conversation with a student's decision to grow with God, many times the cure takes time in coming. I know, though, that we can be assured that as we do our part, God will do his.

Be authentic. Because many students are distrustful of the people who lead them, it is imperative that you place a high priority on loving God visibly and living for him authentically. Your students have seen examples of hypocrisy in the past, and they have no respect for the insincere. However, if they sense that you mean what you say and that you practice what you preach, you will earn their respect and be on your way to influencing their young lives. Don't be afraid to share what you believe with confidence. Students are looking not only for something but also some*one* to believe in.

Be positive. Students who have become too familiar with God have lost sight of the relationship that is available to them. They won't change because they "should" but only if it benefits them, so they must be reminded what this relationship can be in ways that are captivating and attractive. You can't just tell them about the relationship; you must make them see, desire and experience it.

I once told the following story at a camp in Arizona:

I returned home from an extended trip in the middle of the night when everyone was sleeping. The next morning I was up before everyone else, and even though I longed to talk to my wife and hug my children, I snuck downstairs silently so that they could sleep in. After I collected the newspaper from my driveway, I settled into my favorite chair to read. A few minutes later I heard a noise and looked up to see my four-year-old daughter standing in the hallway looking at me with a sweet smile on her face. She did not have to use words to tell me that she was happy to see me home; I just knew. After a brief pause, she walked over to me and crawled under my arm, threw her legs across my lap and put her head on my chest. My father's heart swelled as I put down the paper and just held her. For several minutes we didn't talk. We didn't need to. We just sat there, enjoying each other's company.

After I told that story, a young lady came up to me and quietly admitted, "I want God to hold me like that." Young people who have accepted a nominal faith in place of a vital relationship with God will begin to compare their life with the pictures you paint, and they will long for more. You have succeeded when students begin to approach you and say, "I want to know God like that."

CHANGED HEARTS

Cold and callous hearts can be found in every church. It is often the case that time spent in typical faith-related settings can actually dull students' senses instead of igniting passion for Christ in their hearts. This can happen as familiarity takes the place of hunger and the routine of faith steals the freshness of a real relationship with God. Untold numbers of young people buy into the illusion that everything is fine—but they are being lulled into a deep sleep.

We must see them transformed. We can't be satisfied that they are "good kids." We must work to see them become passionately in love with their Lord. It is the only thing that will protect them from taking their faith for granted. With God's help even the hardest of hearts can be changed.

4

GETTING PAST EXCUSES

When I met Madison at a church camp, she was wearing her dysfunctions like a badge, willing to share them with anyone who would listen. She continually hung around the adults at the camp, seeking their sympathy and affirmation. After every evening message, she went forward for prayer, crying violently. Some of the other students would gather around her to comfort her, even girls who normally avoided her. As you can imagine, this was attention that the insecure and awkward young girl cherished.

Madison was using her personal problems to manipulate others into giving her love and attention, and I knew that something needed to be done. I approached her youth leader, who affirmed my observations and gave me permission to approach Madison with my concerns. Later that afternoon, as we sat on the swings during our "free" time, I didn't berate Madison for her manipulation; instead, I started by asking, "How are you doing spiritually?"

Rather than answer my question directly, she told me how her biological parents had separated when she was five. Although I did not want to trivialize her grief, I was not satisfied with her answer. "But how are you doing in your walk with God?" I asked. Once again, she avoided the question. She shared with me about her hypocritical mother, her abusive stepfather, her family's controlling rules, her youth group that was filled with unloving frauds and her busy schedule that kept her from reading her Bible.

Madison fully expected me to accept her excuses and lather her with sympathy, so she was caught off guard when I continued to press her for a real answer to the question I had asked. Lovingly I challenged her, "Madison, I know that your life has not been perfect. And, for the horrible things that you have experienced I am sorry. However, you still have not answered my question. And I think I know why. I think you have been using all of the things in your past as an excuse to not move forward. When you hurt, God hurts, and he wants to help you overcome those things. You won't be able to do that until you begin to build a healthy spiritual life."

Because she heard the care and concern in my voice, she was willing to hear me out. Madison realized that God was calling her to become one of his children, and together we talked about some of the specific ways that she needed to begin to approach him. I prayed with her for a covering of peace, for protection from harm and for an impartation of spiritual hunger that would drive her into God's presence. I knew that if she would begin to forget what was behind her and press into her future with Christ, she would no longer need to use emotional manipulation to feel loved and accepted.

Madison has written to me a couple of times since that camp, and she seems to be doing well. Now, instead of writing about her horrible life, she is sharing with me the things she is learning from God, and I am picking up the sounds of joy in her voice. Slowly, she is changing, and as she leaves her excuses behind, she will continue to be transformed into the woman God has called her to be.

ANALYZING THEIR ARGUMENTS

Passionate Christians are focused on Christ. Apathetic ones focus on their surroundings, circumstances and barriers instead. Aggressive Christians work to overcome the things that stand in their way. Indifferent Christians make excuses for their problems.

Young people who are not growing in their faith are continually looking for someone or something to blame for their bad attitudes, their addictions to sin and their lack of spiritual progress. Some will blame their heritage ("no one else in my family is a Christian"), while others will blame the hypocrites around them. Some will refuse to look past the pain in their lives, while others will claim that their churches are not relevant to them.

No excuse is a good one. God does not accept them, and we should not either. We must be quick to recognize the blame trend in our students' lives so that we can help them overcome it.

> **"Excuses are the cradle . . . that Satan rocks men off to sleep in."**
>
> **D. L. MOODY**

Because everyone operates differently, we cannot use a blanket statement to describe individuals who hide behind their excuses. However, there are some common characteristics that can help us identify them.

An open book. These students tend to rehearse their problems for anyone who is willing to listen. They zero in on caring adults, and their conversations tend to center around their pasts and their problems. They unload their hurts on others in an attempt to gain attention and affirmation.

Overly empathetic. They also tend to be overly empathetic, seeking out and coddling others who have also had painful experiences. Many times these are the students who love to get in a good cry at every youth event, and although sharing problems can be helpful, going overboard with empathy can actually create unhealthy dependence among these students, preventing them from allowing God to heal their wounds.

Low self-esteem. These students usually have very low self-esteem. Instead of knowing that God is on their side and that with him they can accomplish anything, they wonder if they will ever be anything more than the failures that they have been in the past.

TRIUMPHING OVER THE EXCUSES

Although our society often grades on a curve and pardons those who have had difficult life experiences, our spiritual lives are not evaluated in the same way. All of us, no matter what happened to us in the past, have the choice to trust in Christ and receive everything that he is. When we can help young people get to the point where they no longer offer excuses because they realize that God has something better for them, we will begin to see unprecedented growth made visible by spiritual fruit in their lives. For this to happen we must carry out some strategic actions.

Help them focus forward. It is possible to show genuine care about the pain and difficulties these students have experienced in the past and at the same time encourage them not to dwell on those things. We can pray for them, counsel them and listen to their horrific stories, but our ministry to them must not end there. With carefully chosen words and an anointing that comes from God, we can help them understand that God is bigger than their problems and that the problems are not acceptable excuses for them to stop growing toward God. Instead of letting them focus on the issues of their past, we must point them to their future.

Dwell on the main thing. "He rewards those who earnestly seek him" (Hebrews 11:6). If we want our young people to experience all of God's blessings, we must help them focus on his grace, goodness and love. We must teach them to invest in their spiritual life through their own personal and passionate pursuit of God.

Pastor Scott was good at this. His youth ministry was built around one principle, and it permeated everything he did. He was intent on making sure that his students knew the importance of having daily times with God.

This gifted minister knew that growth would come more quickly through students habitually meeting with God than through any of his creative programming, entertaining messages and communicated love. His experience had taught him that only God could heal wounds, eradicate loneliness and convince of forgiveness, and as a result he taught his students to spend time with God daily. He did not want them to look for his opinions but to long for God's. And he held them accountable for doing so. I can't remember a time that I was with Scott when he didn't look seriously into the eyes of one of his students and ask if he or she had been faithfully doing devotions.

Scott's concern for his students' personal walks with God produced fruit. His church sent a high percentage of mature students on to Bible colleges, missions trips, training programs and effective ministries. His philosophy of ministry is even perpetuated in the youth pastors he has mentored. Just the other day, I heard one of them ask a student if she was faithfully doing her devotions.

Point them to God's comfort. Students will need help overcoming their past if they are to put their excuses aside and start focusing on God. While we can be instrumental in this process, it is even more important that we teach them to let God be their source of comfort.

Bobby Jo loved the attention that she could get from Julie, a youth leader in her church, and she was often moody when she felt she was being ignored. For over a year Julie loved and prayed for Bobby Jo, rushing to her house whenever the phone rang. Eventually, however, Julie realized that Bobby Jo was manipulating her and that, despite her efforts, Bobby Jo had not changed for the better.

Wanting to give Bobby Jo what she needed and not simply what she asked for, Julie began to pray and ask God for heightened discernment. At God's leading, she changed how she acted toward Bobby Jo. Instead of spending hours on the phone with her, Julie would listen sympathetically for a few minutes and then encourage Bobby Jo to run to God. Then she would follow up with a call the next day to see what God had said.

It took several months, but Bobby Jo eventually learned to go vertical with her loneliness, pain and discouragement rather than settle for a horizontal fix. She learned to go to God for affirmation, encouragement and counsel. Now she is being used in her youth group to lead others to Christ. Now she can tell others that authentic and lasting comfort will come from God as he embraces them and loves them more perfectly than any human could.

Make them responsible for their own faith. Although many of our young people would love to blame someone else (their parents or their youth leaders, for example) for their stagnant spiritual life, they can't. They must realize that responsibility for their spiritual walk is theirs and theirs alone.

The Bible says, "Come near to God and he will come near to you" (James 4:8). This promise is for everyone, and it assures us that by simply turning our heart to God and inviting his presence to invade our life, any one of us who wants to be close to him can. The promise also has an opposite effect, for a Christian who does not draw near to God will not have a close walk with him. The bottom line is this: Our relationship with God will be whatever we make it. We must remind our students that he is waiting to be found by them (see Ecclesiastes 12:1; Isaiah 55:6), and that the responsibility is theirs. Hopefully then they will begin to draw close to him.

FROM EXCUSES TO VICTORY

No problem is so big that God will give us a leave of absence from our faith. No amount of abuse, rejection, failure or inadequacy can keep us from having healthy, growing relationships with him. No amount of pain can steal our destinies. Every human being has the opportunity to draw near to God and to experience the comfort, encouragement and power that he can provide. When we effectively teach this to our students, we will see them reject their excuses and their anemic Christianity for a passionate pursuit of the God who is the source of true comfort and satisfaction.

In her early teen years, as the pressures of being in middle school increased, Tina ran from social involvement and avoided spiritual disciplines. In order to escape the pain and awkwardness of adolescence, she became enveloped in every kind of media available to her. In a typical week she saw at least one movie at the theater and watched at least three more on television or video. In the same week she read at least two magazines that promoted worldly approaches to relationships and fashion, and she invested quality time in romance novels that disconnected her from reality. Add to her weekly totals her television habit (especially MTV), the continual noise of her music and her Internet addiction and she had a full plate of entertainment in her life.

Like a child who fills up on snacks and is left with no appetite for the main course, Tina was stripped of her desire to embrace God and his truth because she had dulled her taste to the things that really matter. She thought that escaping into fantasy was a way to make life easier, but that was an illusion. As she lay in bed at night without noise and activity to fill her mind, she was haunted by the truth: Her life was empty, her relationships were superficial, and she didn't know where to turn.

Tina still hides from reality behind a wall of entertainment and avoids the One who can help her deal with her insecurities. Entertainment isolates her from the world and incubates the shame, embarrassment and fears in her life. Until she discovers that a vibrant relationship with Christ will give her a full and victorious life, she will not be willing to move out from behind her wall. If she stays there she will continue to feed the very things that she longs to escape from.

CAUGHT IN THE WEB

Entertainment is a part of our culture, and it is one of the things that compete for our students' time, attention and affections. George Barna, in his book *Real Teens*, points out that

> the influence of the mass media upon the minds and hearts of America's youth cannot be overestimated. Teens spend an average of four to six hours per day interacting with the mass media in various forms. For instance we discovered that 94% listen to the radio, 91% play audiocassettes or compact discs, 89% watch television, 69% read a magazine, 58% read part of a book in a typical day and 52% use the Internet.

Our teens are spending a huge amount of their time immersing themselves in media influences rather than facing the reality of their lives. Not only is the amount of time they invest in these escapist pursuits dangerous; the types of things that they ingest while doing so can also be extremely harmful. Many students who confess that they want to live pure and godly lives spend their time and money on things that contradict their convictions, such as music with profane lyrics, movies with immoral images or magazines with unrealistic and dangerous messages. When teens fill up on these things, their lives are bound to be influenced as a result.

When people become bored with God they seek excitement in other forms.

IDENTIFYING THE CRISIS

Entertainment in and of itself is not wrong, but when teens become addicted to the "noise" all around them, they can enter into a spiritual crisis. Here are three ways that you can identify those students who struggle to balance their spiritual life with their media intake.

They never have time to invest in the things that really matter. They may attend church, confess to love God and claim to be Christians, but their faith is weak because they never invest in it. They lack the desire to pursue spiritual things, but they never lack the craving to be entertained because it takes so little effort and discipline. Their every waking moment is dominated by media as they run to the illusions, excitement and unrealistic values portrayed.

They live in a dream world, searching for a fairy tale that does not exist. These teens are often caught up in the fantasies to which they escape, and they do not deal well with real-life struggles. Instead they run from them, escaping into a movie or song lyrics. But the problems still remain when the noise has quieted; they are not solved in a thirty-minute time slot. The plots of these students' lives can never compare to their make-believe worlds.

They begin to idolize and imitate ungodly people and lifestyles. In many ways, our students are being mentored by media. What they hear in the lyrics of their music and see in the lifestyles of their heroes has an influence on the way they think. The images they see flaunted as desirable become what they "need" in order to find happiness, fulfillment and satisfaction, but the counsel they're receiving is not based on spiritual truth. Rather, it is coming from sources that are casual about or embrace sin.

DANGEROUS ACTIVITIES

Steve and Becky were concerned about their oldest son, Jim. He was engrossed in various types of entertainment, and everything he was drawn to seemed to have a dark side. He and his friends spent many hours in front of video games that promoted excessive violence, and he was fascinated with horror movies. Steve and Becky were beginning to see signs of rebellion and explosive anger in Jim's personality.

Finally, when Jim was fourteen, they decided that they could no longer ignore their concerns. Not knowing where else to turn, they met with their church's youth pastor, who began their meeting by praying for wisdom and asking God to protect Jim's mind from the negative influences he encountered and the destructive attitudes they caused. She ended her prayer by committing Jim to God and asking God to make himself real to the teen. She then told Steve and Becky that it was time for them to have a difficult conversation with their son, to educate him on the dangers that existed, offer new limits to his activities and provide healthy alternatives to his entertainment desires.

When Steve and Becky got home, they gently approached the issue with Jim. "For several months we have been concerned about some of your games and activities, but we didn't know how to approach you about it. But it can't wait any longer. We love you too much to watch you continually put yourself in danger. As your parents it is our job to protect you as much as possible." Steve went on to apologize for ignoring the issue for as long as they had, and although Jim wanted to argue with his parents, their humble yet confident approach to the conversation did not give him an opportunity to raise his voice or aggressively attack.

Over time, the family purged itself of ungodly media and activities, and as Steve and Becky stood their ground and offered reasonable alternatives, Jim argued with them less and less. They also began to make spiritual activities more of a priority, spending time reading and discussing Christian books and praying together before bedtime. As a testimony to God's faithfulness, Jim started to live a more authentic faith. He started to close his door not to avoid his parents but to have privacy so he could connect with his heavenly Father.

COMMUNICATING YOUR CONCERNS

Jim is a perfect example of the fact that it really is possible to break through generational barriers to teach our teens about the negative influences that media can have on them. The key is communication.

Don't wait. Don't wait until the issues rise to a boiling point. Start right now by building relationships in which open and honest conversation is a norm. Make it a habit to initiate discussions about spiritual issues as often as you can. If the line of communication is already open, it will be a valuable tool when the time comes for you to offer correction or direction.

However, if there has been a breach in communication and your concern demands that you have a conversation immediately, then don't wait. Go to the student gently and humbly, communicating your concerns with love. Your

Your concerns and observations must be communicated from your love for the student.

students may at first think that your comments stem from a legalistic or old-fashioned approach to life, but if you persevere and continue to show that you care, they will eventually allow you to talk with them about these issues.

Remind them of their goals. When working with students who you know have a desire to serve and please God, appeal to that longing. Ask them what kind of person they want to be in ten years. "Do you want to be close to God or far away? Do you want your thought life to be godly or immoral?" Then ask, "If you continue to fix your attention on the magazines [or movies or music] that you do, how will that help you achieve your goal?" When you get students think-ing about their spiritual goals to live pure and holy lives, you can help them realize the dangerous influences that entertainment can have.

Remember to listen. Don't forget that communication is twofold. You must not just share your thoughts; you must also hear theirs. By asking them questions, you will learn what they think, which will help you understand and directly address the errors in their beliefs—and they may even tell you something that will set your mind at ease.

Do the research. There are two approaches to discussing issues of concern with your students. You can sit down with them and evalu-ate the content of magazines, books, music, videos or movies to-gether. For example, you might read a song's lyrics together or ask di-rect questions like, "What was that movie trying to convince you of?" Or, you can do your own research and investigate the various forms of media and their overall messages before you have the conversa-tion. If you do the research on your own, you will be able to talk in-telligently and specifically about the materials instead of making un-informed statements and endangering your students' respect for you.

Encourage realistic evaluation. As you talk with them, try to get them to be honest with themselves about the influences that they are subjecting themselves to. As much as they would love to use logical arguments to support their habits, sometimes their opinions are based simply on preferences and not on facts. As they talk they may come to the realization that their views are incorrect and their habits dangerous.

Forget your own agenda. In addition, remember that your con-versation is not about your personal preferences and comfort zones either. Rather, it should be about biblical principles and strategies for spiritual growth. Don't go into conversations planning to have a battle of opinions; instead, work to highlight the values that will protect the hearts of your students and aid them in pursuing God.

BUCK'S STORY

Buck was quite a kid. He was outgoing and loud, and there was never a dull moment when he was around. He had grown up in the church, but most of his relationships were with boys who were not believers. Buck loved God and wanted to be more like him, but his friendships led him into dangerous places. He was so busy with his friends that he neglected to spend a regular quiet time with God, and the movies they watched fed his lustful thoughts. He occasionally felt grief over the fact that his spiritual life was so weak, but he rarely had time to think about deep things.

Then at a Sunday morning church service something clicked for Buck. The pastor made a passing comment that the Holy Spirit directed toward Buck's heart. He simply said, "The strength of your life will be discovered in the secret place."

For hours, Buck mulled that over; he began to pray and seek God's heart. He recalled something a youth speaker had once said: "If your spiritual life is going to improve, you are going to have to change the way that you approach the world, and you are going to have to change the way that you approach God." Buck knew what he had to do. He was going to have to guard his heart from all of the nasty influences in his life, and he was going to have to spend more time pursuing God. Realizing that his time was a precious commodity, he began to invest it instead of wasting it.

Today, Buck is doing very well spiritually. He is a pastor of a small church and a family man, and he is still pursuing Christ. On occasion he enjoys a movie with his family, but he is selective about what he watches and how much time he spends being entertained. He guarded his heart and pursued God, and it changed his life. Now he is fulfilling his destiny.

GUARD THEIR HEARTS

We are often fighting an uphill battle as we seek to help our students understand the severity of the consequences of their choices. According to the Kaiser Family Foundation's survey of 503 teens ages fifteen to seventeen, 72 percent of the respondents said that they thought sexual content on television influences other teens' sexual behavior either "a lot" or "somewhat." However, 78 percent said that it had little or no impact on their own behavior. As objective outsiders, we realize the dangerous effects of media, but from the inside our teens are oblivious.

We must fervently pray that God will teach our young people to guard their hearts (see Proverbs 4:23) against the negative influences in the world, to give them the wisdom and confidence to walk away when they are confronted by something that should offend or embarrass them. And we must be his instruments in teaching them to discern what is constructive and what is dangerous.

Our students are set apart for God. They are called to love him and to love only the things that he loves. Achieving these goals may mean limiting certain forms of entertainment that would try to lead them astray and avoiding others altogether. If they are to be addicted, may it be only to the presence of God. If they need to "escape," may it be into his love and grace.

Michael had a tremendous ability to avoid people, especially those who could see through his façade. I met him at a camp, and right away it was obvious to me that he felt awkward and longed to fit in with his peers. He tried desperately to be the center of attention, but the kids around him just rolled their eyes and walked away. In addition, Michael was addicted to pornography. The shame and embarrassment that he felt about his secret life further stripped him of his dignity and self-esteem. When he discovered that his youth pastor knew what was going on in his life, Michael started avoiding him. Michael was obviously hurting, but he refused to receive help because he wouldn't let anyone get close to him.

At the camp, I watched Michael avoid his youth pastor for two days before I finally pulled him aside and encouraged him to seek accountability. I told him that his youth pastor would be a great resource to help him overcome his struggles. Michael pretended to take my counsel, but as soon as our talk was over, the walls went right back up. To this day, he refuses to let his youth pastor be a part of his life. Michael wants to be in full-time youth ministry, yet he refuses to come out of hiding and deal with the issues in his life.

YOU CAN RUN BUT YOU CAN'T HIDE

People may not be pleased with their sin and immaturity, but often they are too detached to put forth an honest effort to see those things change. Instead they isolate themselves from the people in their life who may challenge them on these issues, and they work overtime to keep their relationships on shallow levels so that their sin is not discovered. The reasons they hide vary, but several symptoms are common among people who struggle in this area.

Unhealthy self-perception. Much of their behavior is driven by the question, "Would they love me if they really knew me?" Because their self-worth is tied up in their accomplishments or their appearances, they are overly concerned about putting the right foot forward. When they don't perform up to their standards or when their flaws are revealed, they don't like what they see when they look in the mirror. They begin to question their value as human beings and pull away from others to make sure that no one has the opportunity to judge them. Struggling to believe that people could care about them in their imperfect state makes them also doubt that God could love them. As a result, they struggle to love themselves.

Difficulty overcoming sins. The habit of keeping everyone at a distance prevents these people from receiving strength, prayers and assistance from those around them. As a result, they struggle to conquer their addictions and defeat their failures. Like a drowning man who is all alone, they have no one to help pull them ashore or share the burden of staying afloat.

Loneliness. Although their loneliness is self-inflicted, it is still awkward, painful and damaging. They wonder why they don't have any real friends and believe that no one likes them. The truth is that they have isolated themselves socially so well and for so long that few have the patience to attempt to break through the barriers to reach them.

Bottled emotions. People who won't let anyone get close to them hide their pain until it explodes. The sad thing is that this could be prevented if they are aware of the dangers of keeping others at a distance. When they put on their disguises and pretend that they are happy and satisfied with life, others are surprised when they finally lose control. I believe that the groundwork for many suicides and violent crimes is laid when individuals decide to keep others at a distance.

SAY GOODBYE TO SECLUSION

Nothing good happens when people are allowed to put up unhealthy barriers and keep others at a distance. They may seem to take nothing seriously, or they may hide behind bitterness and anger, but meanwhile their despair is being incubated and gaining strength. As the Bible says, "Even in laughter the heart may ache, and joy may end in grief" (Proverbs 14:13).

Because this kind of isolation is dangerous if it is allowed to go on unhindered, we must be proactive and intentional about recognizing and addressing these tendencies in our students' lives. When you recognize that a student is trying to hide from you, don't overlook it; point out his or her behavior.

Some of the people who habitually hide from others don't even realize that they do it. When you confront them, give specific examples of the behavior you've observed. For example, you might say, "Kelsey, why do you avoid having conversations with people on the bus?" or "Steve, I have noticed that when I try to have a conversation with you about your spiritual life, you get grumpy and tell me that you aren't in the mood to talk." Don't allow them to continue to run. Remind them that while God does not expect perfection, we still must strive to live holy lives, and we cannot hide from him.

DOUG'S STORY

While some students are not aware that they have been hiding, others have strategically crafted walls to keep you out because they know that you will challenge them in their sin.

Doug was such a student. When I heard rumors that he was pursuing a physical relationship with one of our young girls, I asked him to meet with me to talk. He made excuses about scheduling conflicts, but I found a hole in his crafted defense and set up a time to meet with him.

Our conversation began directly. "How are you and Lynn doing?" I asked. Casually he responded, "Good." But then I pressed further with questions like, "How are you doing spiritually? Are you protecting her physically, or are you two going past godly boundaries?" and his confidence waned. The more we talked the quieter he became.

"Listen, Doug," I said. "You know I love you. I know that God is calling you to take a stand for him and be a leader. That starts with your most sacred relationships. When you push the physical limits in your relationship with Lynn, you aren't protecting her. You are damaging her." Something I said hit a nerve, and Doug admitted that he had been feeling the conviction of the Holy Spirit recently, but he had ignored it. He confessed that he had avoided me and the other youth leaders because he was afraid that we would judge him for his sin or try to help him change.

"Doug," I said, "you have to decide if you want to live for God and please him. If you do, then it is time that you begin to pursue him and let him change you." At that point, Doug admitted that he wanted to be close to God no matter what the cost. After another hour of conversation, we left with a plan for him to bring accountability into his spiritual life and his relationships with others. A couple of weeks later, Doug and Lynn broke up, and he is now on a steady path in pursuit of Christ.

ONE BRICK AT A TIME

Even though we desire to see all of our conversations work as well as
the one I had with Doug, the truth is that many times they do not. Usually it takes patience and persistence to see the walls coming down.

Although Kayla had grown up with parents who loved her and encouraged her to fall in love with Christ, her apathy toward spiritual
things pulled her away from her mom and dad as well as from all
spiritual activity and healthy relationships. She began to choose new
friends who had authority problems and strong addictions, and her
parents began to get nervous. They tried talking to her about their
concerns, but she would walk out of the room the moment she
sensed that the conversation was turning serious.

When Kayla ended up in the hospital to have her stomach
pumped after a drug overdose, the tension in her family jumped to a
new level. Her parents tried to have a serious talk with her, but Kayla
refused to listen and yelled and cursed at them.

A week later her parents found themselves in the youth pastor's
office. Knowing that he could not fix the situation, the youth pastor
offered support and committed to pray for Kayla. He encouraged
them to continue trying to engage her in conversation, to build a relationship with her and to do family activities that she enjoyed.
Kayla's parents committed to doing these things, and while they did
not force anything on her, they tried to gently build a relationship
with their daughter. As a result they began to see signs that Kayla's
wall was beginning to crumble.

Finally, one morning before school Kayla came down the stairs and
found her mom sitting at the table reading her Bible. For a minute she
stood there in silence, and then she spoke. "Mom, how do you know
that God is there?" From there a conversation took off that led to
Kayla's rededication to Christ. Kayla's problems didn't go away imme-

diately, but after a season of struggle, she was a completely different person. It didn't happen overnight, but the walls came down as those who loved her prayed faithfully and held on to hope.

FENDING OFF PERSONAL ATTACKS

Not only must you persevere as you wait for students' walls to crumble; you must also persist when the tactics students use to keep you at a distance become personal. Sometimes young people lash out in aggressive attacks, shouting things like "I hate you!" or "Why won't you get a clue and leave me alone?" to the people who are trying to reach out to them. It is important for you to fight off your hurt or frustration and realize that your students' words and actions are being used by the enemy to drive a wedge between the one who needs the help and the one who can offer it.

One summer afternoon, one of my interns and I took Paul and his friend out to play basketball. We tried to get into a conversation that ran deeper than basketball, but Paul wouldn't allow it. After a few hours of hanging out, our time together ended with high fives and a "See you tomorrow."

The next day Paul showed up at the youth service alone and with a quirky smile on his face. I greeted him and told him that I had enjoyed our time together, but his comments weren't as kind. "Sean, I hate to tell you this, but my friend liked Shawn (my intern) better than you." Waiting for a reaction, he stood there with a smile on his face.

I have to admit that my first reaction was to be offended. *That's just great. I go out of my way to hang out with this scrawny kid, and his friend hates me.* But knowing that Paul wanted me to react that way, I went the other direction. "That's awesome! Hey Shawn, come here. Paul's friend thought you were cool! Way to go!" Paul stood there with a shocked look on his face. He was obviously confused that his attempt to scar me actually brought me joy.

OUT OF HIDING

As you deal with students who are trying to distance themselves from you, pray for wisdom and discernment. Instead of blurting out words that are influenced by your emotions, frustrations and personal biases, wait for words that God inspires. When you speak God's words, not one of them will miss their mark (see Isaiah 55:11).

When praying, don't forget to ask God to make your students desperate for him (see Psalm 42:1-2), and seek the opinions and assistance of others who are spiritual influences in your students' lives. By doing so you will have companions who can agree with you in prayer for your students and assist you in ambushing them with love and affirmation.

We have all known people who were embarrassed by their failures.

Some students seem to be asking for a rebuke and a reprimand, but that is not what they really need. What they need is acceptance and affirmation. When they try to keep you away, they seem to be instigating your anger, but what they need is to know that you still love them despite their failures. They need you in their life, and they need you to inspire them toward spiritual growth. As you find ways to coax them out of hiding and encourage them to grow in their relationship with God, you will see them becoming the people God truly intends for them to be.

7

HELPING THEM UP
AFTER THEY HAVE FALLEN

When I was a teen I had a friend named Troy who was surrounded by all the good things that most "church kids" have: Christian parents, a church that was trying to be relevant to his generation, friends who were moral and a youth pastor who was constantly reaching out to him. Yet despite all of this, Troy was still searching for meaning in his life.

Our youth pastor inspired us with his passionate love for Christ, but that kind of faith didn't seem realistic to Troy. His failures convinced him that he could never have faith like that. His relationship with God was a distant memory when he was away from the church environment, he had trouble controlling his temper and cheated on tests, and lustful thoughts dominated his mind. Rather than run to God for help, Troy hid from him out of guilt. Eventually he gave up trying to have a faith like our youth pastor's. His Christianity had become a reminder of his failures instead of a tool that freed him to live righteously before God.

During a vulnerable moment after a church service Troy asked me the question that had been haunting him: "Why am I even trying to live for Christ? I am never going to be able to do it right." Being a teenager myself, I didn't know how to answer his question, and I watched helplessly as my friend agonized over his own weaknesses and past failures. He was buried beneath the weight of disappointment and frustration, and he couldn't see a way out.

WHEN FAILURE BECOMES A HABIT

Failure is both a consequence and a cause of apathy. When Christians allow spiritual boredom to creep into their lives and are no longer seeking and submitting to God's will, they will begin to make bad decisions that result in failure. That failure then causes them to reason, "If I can't stand, what is the use in trying?" and strengthens the apathy that caused the failure in the first place.

I am convinced that there are more of today's Christian young people who are frustrated with their spiritual development than there are those who are flat-out rebellious. Schools and churches everywhere are filled with students who are bound by pasts that are littered with weakness and failure.

In order to help these students, we must see past their exteriors to their hearts and learn to recognize the intentional and unintentional patterns they get into. If we do not point them beyond their mistakes, their failures could haunt them forever.

They will have no energy for pursuing God. Failure has a way of sapping the strength out of a person. It invites fatigue and a sense of helplessness, which can be interpreted by others as complacency. We must realize that students who seem like they no longer want to try may simply be too tired to reach out for help.

They will be dominated by negative emotions. Feeling like a failure tends to steal all of the joy and peace out of a life. The emotions these students feel, such as depression, anger and insecurity, are negative and destructive. They define, dominate and steal hope from our students, preventing them from being able to feel happy or content.

They will compare themselves to others—unrealistically. These students are so aware of their own weaknesses that all they can see is how poorly they compare to everyone around them. Instead of hearing encouraging words that will help them get back on track or realizing that no one is perfect, all they can see is that everyone else seems so together and they are not.

They will avoid places where God might speak to them. Young people who are overcome by their failures will do whatever it takes to avoid conviction, whether that is daydreaming or talking out loud during a youth service or finding ways to avoid the situations altogether. If their churches are places where God's Spirit convicts people of sin and encourages them to run after God, these students will become less faithful in their attendance. If they have had mountaintop experiences at camps or conferences in the past yet have failed to follow through on the commitments they made, they will not want to attend the camps again. They may have what sound like good excuses, but many times it comes down to the fact that they are hiding from God so that they will not be reminded of past failures or encouraged to change their life.

They may attack others who are trying to live right. Unknowing and sincere Christians who are working hard to live right before God often serve to amplify the guilt of those students who are bound by their failures. When these students see others who are walking in the strength that they long for, they have difficulty being happy for those people and often attempt to undermine their confidence by attacking their convictions and deflating their joy. Yet, all the while these students are disappointed in themselves for losing the very things they are criticizing the others for having.

They will continue to fall hard. When students become consumed by their own failures, they reason that if they can't live for God without failure, they shouldn't even try anymore. They might as well have all of the fun that they can. Students who believe this lie are likely to fall hard and fast.

KICKING THE EFFECTS OF FAILURE TO THE CURB

Students who are bound by their failures are everywhere. They are tragically walking away from the spiritual foundations that have been built into their lives, and in doing so influencing others to walk into dangerous places with them. Many of them will return after a season of straying, but even so they will carry with them scars from that time away. We must help these students overcome their failures and move into victorious lives in Christ.

Don't interpret their frustration as rebellion. It is easy to confuse frustrated students with rebellious ones. The two different types must be handled differently, so it's important to learn to recognize the difference between them. You can determine whether a student is frustrated or truly rebellious by asking one question: "If it was easy to get there, what would you want your spiritual life to look like?" If the student honestly responds, "I want to walk closely with God and obey him in all things," then you have something to work with. However, if the response is, "I don't want to live for God. I want to do my own thing," then you are dealing with a rebel. Rebelliousness demands confrontation, but young people who are frustrated need patience, kindness and encouragement.

Love them. People who are overshadowed by their own mistakes tend to be very hard on themselves and feel that they are not worthy of love. Love, however, is exactly what they need if they are going to overcome their struggles with the past, and they need to see it demonstrated in real and practical ways. Make time to take them somewhere special, send them cards, slip notes under their windshield wipers or send them pictures of the two of you together with a thought written on the back of them. (Be careful to communicate appropriately and to be sensitive to the signals they send you. The goal is to make them feel safe.) These are small expressions, but they will mean a lot. When you demonstrate love to these students, you are proving that it is possible for God to love them too.

Be vulnerable with them. All of us have failed. We have made commitments to God, and we have struggled to see them through. I am always amazed at Paul's public confessions of his weaknesses. He actually boasted about his failures (see 2 Corinthians 12:7-10). I believe that Paul knew he was writing to imperfect people who needed to hear that it was normal to be imperfect and that there was hope.

It is difficult to share our failures with others, but it is these glimpses into our human sides that will encourage our students to keep trying. If they think that we have always been strong, they will be discouraged by their own weaknesses. If they see someone who has struggled and overcome difficulties, they will have hope.

By sharing your struggles you help them relate to you and believe that they can get to where you are.

Concentrate on direction over perfection. Immature Christians often believe that God will not accept someone who is imperfect, and many times spiritual leaders add to the pressure students feel by placing unrealistic expectations on them. While we must be certain to teach our students God's standards for righteousness, we must also help them understand his grace that overcomes our shortcomings. God knows that our journeys will be long and that we will never reach perfection. Instead of focusing on perfection we need to point our students in the right direction and assure them that God will be with them along the way.

Speak hope. Failure strips people of their ability to believe that things can ever get better. As leaders functioning in a world of hopelessness, we must resurrect hope and point our students to the future. Remember, God has said that he is "able to keep you from falling and to present you before his glorious presence without fault and with great joy" (Jude 24). Use these words of hope to encourage students who long to overcome their failures. Show them that with God's help it is possible for them to overcome their past and carve out a great future.

People who fail to communicate God's mercy will repel those who need to be reached.

Teach them to pray God's promises. Students who have been ambushed by failure need a crash course on praying God's promises for their life. Here are a few examples of how they can pray the powerful Word of God in personal ways.

> God, I thank you that no temptation is bigger than you. I know that you will not let me be tempted beyond what I can bear. You will always give me a way out, so that I can stand up under the trials I face (1 Corinthians 10:13).

> May the words of my mouth and the thoughts I think be pleasing to you, O God (Psalm 19:14).

> God, you said that I am righteous before you (2 Corinthians 5:21) and that you are able to keep me from falling into sin (Jude 24). Help me to live up to what I have already attained (Philippians 3:16).

> God's Word is powerful (see Hebrews 4:12), and when we can get our students praying his promises, they will receive a newfound confidence and learn to release his power through their prayers.

POINTED TOWARD VICTORY

Many of the students we have invested in, prayed for and labored with are being shackled by their own failures. They may be inspired by the lives of others who have freedom in Christ, but they don't know how to achieve the same success and are drowning in a pool of frustration. As their leaders, it is our job to show them that through the blood of Christ they can move past their failures and begin walking toward confidence, stability and victory in him. When they realize this they will rise up with renewed energy and focus their eyes not on themselves but on the God who desires to bring them to ultimate completion.

8

When they arrived at the camp for at-risk students, they had no idea what they were in for, but they quickly found out. The very first thing they discovered was that all of their rights had been revoked. Their luggage was searched, and all alcohol, tobacco products and illegal drugs were confiscated. Not only that, but revealing clothing and makeup were removed from the girls' suitcases as well.

A few of the students tried to reason with the staff, while others used foul language and threatened violence. Although their reactions were diverse, their surprise was universal. *How dare they?* they thought.

These teens' parents had entrusted their kids to this particular Christian organization and given permission for the staff to use whatever means were necessary to bring the teens around. Although the students did not appreciate the limitations that were placed on them, the staff was not interested in personal convenience or comfort. They were interested in maturity.

WHEN THEIR RIGHTS MEAN TOO MUCH

When spiritual apathy sneaks into students' lives, their desire to please God and live according to his standards weakens. Instead of craving holiness, they settle for comfort, and personal preference takes the place of submission. They become determined to "hold on to their rights" and will fight for the things they desire, ignoring the standards that they know God has set for them.

Recently I read an article about a musician who claimed to know Christ but who had made a name for herself on the R&B scene by singing about sexual encounters. When her interviewer asked how she could justify the hypocrisy in her life, she responded, "Oh, I love Jesus. I just like giddy-up (sex) also." When people say that they love God but are not willing to abide by his commands, they are holding on to their rights too tightly. When they rationalize their sin, they are choosing their own desires over God's. This communicates to those around them that Christianity is not about Christ but about self.

These people tend to be defensive and argumentative when their choices are questioned. Although they may defend their faith, you can be sure that they will also go to great lengths to defend what they believe to be their rights. They would rather argue than listen to the convicting things that others have to say. Their goal is not to discover the truth but to protect their opinions.

The gifts God has stored up for us are richer than the things we can gather on our own.

Because they hold so firmly to their rights and to their way of life, they miss out on the blessings that God desires to give them. Recently a friend of mine, David, admitted to me that he had held off God's best while he was looking out for his own rights. In high school he had made his own choices and lived in ways that he knew were contrary to God's call on his life. When David finally recommitted himself to Christ, God began a process of refining and directing him. He realizes now that when he gave up his rights and gave God the control, his faith became real and his life became more fulfilling. David is so glad that he made the choice to give God complete access to his life. He only wishes that he had done it sooner.

LOOSENING THEIR GRIP

Our rights are often what prevents us from becoming mature Christians. Teens' right to choose their own friends may keep them from spiritual growth if the friends they choose are not positive influences on their lives. Their right to choose their own entertainment may feed sinful thoughts and desires in their hearts if what they choose promotes ungodly ideas.

No choice is meaningless or insignificant.

We must teach young people that yielding their rights to the Lord will allow them to enjoy the benefits of having made wise choices. Only when we submit to God will we find protection, fulfillment and provision. Only then will we allow him to give us everything he is so desperate to bless us with. Moses had a choice to either hold on to his right to live like royalty and enjoy worldly power or to give up his rights for his convictions (see Hebrews 11:24). By choosing the latter he discovered his destiny.

Look to the future. Most students are trapped in the present and struggle to make decisions based on the unknown future. We must make it clear to them that every choice they make lays a brick on the structure of their life (see 1 Corinthians 10:23). If we can teach them that the decisions they make now affect who they will become, then they may rethink the rights they so zealously defend.

Paint a clear picture. The word *submission* generally carries a negative connotation in today's society, so when we talk about giving up our rights, we have to do more than just tell students that they should submit to Christ. We must paint a clear picture of submission and model it in our own lives so our students know what it looks like. By giving them clear and relevant examples of what we mean, we can show them that submission to God is not stifling or impossible but feasible and beneficial.

Talk about hypocrisy. Because there is something deep inside of us that tells us we should do what we say and live what we believe, even nominal believers have strong feelings about hypocrisy. Talk with your students about famous personalities who seem to live ungodly lives and yet thank God in every award speech. Ask the students their opinions, and then take the conversation to a personal level. Ask them, "Do you see any hypocrisy in your own life? How do you think God feels about that?" The goal of this conversation should not be to make accusations but to apply godly principles to our lives on a personal level.

Follow the intent, not just the rule. Instead of just obeying the rules for their own sake or to avoid punishment, we must help students consider the intent behind God's commands. For example, his intent for us is purity, so instead of just asking, "How far is too far?" ask, "How close can I stay to purity?" Society teaches us that we only have to obey authority when the consequences of disobedience are extreme, but God teaches us to obey the purpose behind the mandates. Real submission means submitting to God's heart, not just his words.

Speak up and then let God work. Students will not make progress in this area without the Holy Spirit working in their life, so I am not suggesting that you can develop such a talent at conversation that you can actually persuade them just by speaking to them. However, the goal of your conversations should be to communicate these truths; then you can leave the results of what you said to God. As you walk in submission to him, the things you say will have weight because of the authority you have in Christ.

Pray first. I recently had a conversation with Nicholi, whose defiant seventeen-year-old daughter Ashley was involved in a dating relationship that her mother had not known about, was going to parties behind her mom's back and had started smoking. Nicholi told me that the first thing she did when she found out about Ashley's secrets was pray. It was not a prayer of great faith, but one of "Oh God, what is going on?"

But as Nicholi and her husband sought God's guidance, that desperate cry for help turned into a prayer of confidence that he was in control of the situation. It went something like this: "Right now, we take a stand against all of the powers of the enemy that are attacking our daughter and our family. We stand in God's anointing, and we take the authority that has been given to us by God to lead this family. We refuse to let rebellion and lies drag our daughter away. God, give us wisdom. Help us to communicate with our daughter and take the blinders off of her eyes. Protect her, draw her closer to you and bring our little girl back into submission first to you and then to us."

With confidence, they entered Ashley's room right before bedtime and told her that they knew about her behavior. When Ashley tried to argue with them, they refused to hear it. The conversation went on for quite some time, but it ended with hugs and tears. Ashley admitted that she had been hiding things from her parents and asked for forgiveness. Their relationship became much more open, and now Ashley is doing well and getting more involved in spiritual pursuits.

Although I love the end of the story, I also love the middle. Nicholi knew that it wasn't great parenting that had made Ashley hear them out and realize that her rebellion was wrong. She knew that it was the spiritual authority they had received from God as they asked for his wisdom and direction that overcame Ashley's combative spirit. Remember to always fight for your students in the spiritual arena before you ever try to confront them in a verbal way.

TEACHING THEM TO STAND ASIDE

Because God's first concern for our students is not their convenience or comfort but their maturity, he will occasionally need to ask them to give up their rights. Chances are some of them will squirm under the pressure and run from the conviction. Some will hold on to their rights much more tightly than they will embrace God's plan. Others, however, will learn to relinquish their rights to God and find themselves better off for having done so. When they stand aside and allow God to go through their luggage they will begin to mature.

Tom was gifted, outgoing and funny, and his charismatic personality gave him an almost idol status among the younger kids in the youth group. Yet Tom abused the position he held by ignoring the responsibility that came with it. Instead of being a positive role model, he modeled a disregard for God and his Word that affected the spiritual lives of his peers. Instead of actively participating in worship and attentively listening to the messages being given, he entertained the people around him so that no one else was focused either. The more direct the message was the more he squirmed. When God's conviction was strong, Tom would use every trick in his arsenal to remove the bright spotlight that was shining on his soul.

I loved Tom for his energy, but it frustrated me that he was unwilling to use his gifts in the ways God had intended for them to be used. It was bad enough that Tom was running from God, but it was even worse that the resulting distractions stole the attention of many others in the group as well.

WATCHING THEM SQUIRM

When students shift their energy away from pursuing God, many times that same energy is then redirected into avoiding God altogether. When conviction begins to hit these students' hearts, they must make a move to relieve the pressure and break the sincerity of the moment. Sometimes that means that they fidget and squirm when God comes near, and often that squirming affects the others around them. They may tap someone, crack a joke or noticeably roll their eyes. Although it would be easy to write off all such disruptions as "normal" for that age group (and sometimes they are), we must realize that many times distraction is a specific strategy designed to avoid conviction.

While at a camp in Ohio I met a youth pastor's son who was a spiritual squirmer. Although he was eighteen years old, he had the attention span of a twelve-year-old. During every service he talked, made sounds and fidgeted. During one service he even pulled out his cell phone and started to play a game. Although the majority of the audience was listening and responding as God spoke to them, this young man seemed to refuse to pay attention.

During an evening service I was speaking about shame and how it is caused by sin in our lives. As I told stories of people who were paralyzed by their past, I looked over to see this young man becoming more distracted and trying to steal his friends' attention from my message. I realized that he was trying to avoid the pressure of the spotlight that was shining on his own soul. As God gave me direction, I addressed the group: "As we talk about this intense subject, some of you are going to get very uncomfortable. As you realize that the topic is very real in your lives, you may want to avoid the sense that you are being exposed. But I need you to pay attention and not squirm. Don't talk. Don't get up and go to the bathroom. Just sit there and let God speak to you. I promise you that the only reason that God would invade these deep and hidden parts of your life is because he wants to bring forgiveness and healing to you."

It worked. The young man sat still and seemed to pay attention as I finished my talk. When I gave an opportunity to respond, he did not wait but moved to the front of the room immediately. As I approached, he hugged me and began to share about his past failure in a relationship. Tears flowed as he shared the guilt that he felt. That night God encountered that young man, convinced him that he was forgiven and called him out as a leader. From that night on he aggressively worshiped and encouraged his friends to seek God.

Just like this student, many times the most gifted and influential students are the ones who squirm away from God's conviction in their life. Although they have God-given leadership abilities, they misuse them and lead others away from God instead of to him. Yet when these students submit to God's leading, they can become some of our greatest assets. For the sake of these students and the others around them, we must address this spiritual "squirminess."

TAKING THE WIGGLE OUT OF THE WORM

Students who strategically squirm have honed their ability to not answer questions. They will protect their private lives at all costs and intentionally keep leaders at a distance. Many times they will use humor to avoid direct questions. Some of these young people have been practicing their evasion tactics for years. They know how to sit in a room where God is speaking and not hear a thing.

Unfortunately, ministering to these students can be an uphill battle, since it often means chasing after young people who do not want to be caught. The devil has worked to blind their generation, keeping them numb and apathetic, and he has done his job well. But do not be discouraged. "The one who is in you is greater than the one who is in the world" (1 John 4:4). God is in the business of catching up with people who are running from him (look at Jonah), speaking to people who do not believe his claims (Saul of Tarsus) and placing a healthy passion for himself in people who were once self-centered (Peter). Here are a few suggestions to help you get started with leading your students in the right direction.

Show them who they are. Unless students recognize their weaknesses, they won't let God encounter them. By helping them take a look in the mirror, you can encourage them to open up to the conviction of God's Spirit.

It can help if you share your own testimony or tell a story with a relatable character. For example, when I told the story of a girl who began to doubt that God could love her with all of her faults, not a sound could be heard from the audience—even the ones who were chronic squirmers. When I told about a girl who dealt with extreme loneliness and used to cry herself to sleep, **God knows your** all eyes were focused on me. When you **students.** discover ways to give students a glimpse in the mirror, you will see them begin to long to be different. When you engage them on that level, they will listen.

Control the distractions. When we choose to ignore distractions rather than confront them, we are giving permission for that behavior to continue. When you see young people talking, goofing off or sleeping through youth services, take action. Say something like, "Hey guys, listen up! I know that some of you are starting to squirm, but you need to hear this." Or make eye contact with the young people who are causing the distraction. Whatever you do (try to avoid embarrassing the students), make it clear that it is time to pay attention. You can be sure that you will offend some students as you weed out distractions, but you will also discover that there are others who are grateful that you are finally taking a stand.

Speak with conviction. "Preach the Word; be prepared in season and out of season; correct, rebuke and encourage—with great patience and careful instruction" (2 Timothy 4:2). In this verse Paul isn't just addressing the activity of preaching but also the attitude behind it, and the same is relevant for us as we attempt to lead our students in the right direction. Conviction dominates inattention. When your students see that you mean what you say, they will take notice. When they realize that you are sharing information that affects their lives, they will listen.

Let them see your struggles and the doubts you have overcome. They will see that they can relate to you, and they'll learn that you're worth listening to.

Keep chipping away. These students may not want to be pursued, but it is truly what they need. Don't give up. You never know which conversation, sermon or question will trigger something in their heart.

Candice came to church because her parents made her go and because there were boys there, but she struggled to hear what God was saying to her. Though I was frustrated with her lack of response, I knew that some day God would get through to her, so I kept trying to reach her.

Then one morning Candice's mom called me and told me that when Candice had come home from our youth service the night before, she couldn't stop talking about the neat things that God had done at the meeting. Confused, I thought back to the previous night. She hadn't acted any differently. She hung around the boys, refused to participate in the worship, seemed vacant during the message and remained seated during the altar call. "What exactly did she say?" I asked.

Her mom told me that Candice had been reminded about God's love for her when, as she was leaving, I patted her on the head and told her that God loved her. I didn't know whether I should be thrilled for her breakthrough or mad that I had wasted so much time. All it took was a pat on the head and a common phrase to really impact her.

Don't ever lose hope and don't ever stop doing the right thing. "Let us not become weary in doing good, for at the proper time we will reap a harvest if we do not give up" (Galatians 6:9).

Rely on the Holy Spirit to do his work. The Bible teaches that it is through God's will and his work in peoples' lives (no matter their ages, maturity levels or rating on the squirm meter) that people learn to reject the wrong things, embrace the right ones and be positive influences on others. With authority you can pray Titus 2:11-12 for your students: "For the grace of God that brings salvation has appeared to my teenagers. It teaches them to say 'No' to ungodliness and worldly passions, and to live self-controlled, upright and godly lives in this present age."

MOVING SQUIRMERS TOWARD SUBMISSION

Unless our students let God speak to the deep areas of their heart, they will not grow. If they hide from things deep and spiritual, they will be weak and anemic in their faith, for nothing healthy grows in that environment. We must encourage them to overcome the urge to squirm and instead submit to God's leading in their life. Only then will we see them using their God-given gifts as they were intended and making an impact on those around them.

10

When Paul rolled into work one Saturday morning he was unusually happy. I had become so used to him stumbling in angry and depressed that I was caught off-guard by his smile and his desire to talk. Although we had grown up in the same church, our lives had taken totally different directions. I had decided to walk with God, and Paul had not. He was living for the thrill of the immediate moment, which usually led to trouble and guilt in the next.

As we began to talk that day, Paul was eager to share with me what he had done the night before. He had been at a party and found himself in a back room sharing a joint with a friend. Proudly, Paul told me, "In between hits, I told him that Jesus loved him."

In frustration I blurted out, "Paul, don't you understand what you are doing? When your lifestyle and your words don't match up, you are promoting Jesus in a way that he doesn't want to be promoted. Until you are at least trying to live for God, don't talk about him to other people."

SOMETHING IS MISSING

Paul represents so many students in the church today. They have become convinced that Christianity can be compartmentalized and accessed whenever convenient. They feel that they can have a life of faith but ignore most of God's commands. They are morally apathetic even if on occasion they are evangelistically hungry.

Students who don't value holiness will rationalize sin until they feel justified in it. Some will even go so far as to directly defy Scripture, claiming that it is outdated and not relevant to their life. They tend to be gossip hounds, quick to point out others' weaknesses to remove the spotlight from themselves. They accuse parents and leaders of having unrealistic expectations and of judging them, implying that they can't or don't want to live up to those standards. When these students creep into a church or youth group, they can be more destructive than a nonbeliever off of the street, because as they hide behind their religious façades, they are all the while influencing others with their addictions and rationalizations.

Denise and Barb had been leaders in my youth group for about two years, and they attended a local Christian school. Right in the middle of their high school years their spiritual focus became blurred and their priorities shifted. Suddenly they wanted to try everything that was trendy and experience everything that the world had to offer. One day we got into a conversation with some of the other students about parties, alcohol and dating. Barb began to grow defensive and said, "Just because we are Christians, people expect us to be perfect. I hate the fact that we have to live by higher and more unrealistic standards than everyone else."

I was completely caught off-guard that this had become personal. I had no idea that Barb (and Denise) had been partying, experimenting with alcohol and playing games in the area of sexuality (they were quick to state that they were both still virgins). As we talked, they didn't want to discuss their activities in light of what was right and wrong. They wanted to hide behind the fact that no one is perfect. They had bunkered in behind their excuses, and their defiant attitudes said, "I am going to do whatever I want, no matter what anyone else—even God—might say."

Barb and Denise were very fortunate; they pulled out of their nose-dive before anything major happened. Although in later years they had to deal with the guilt of their choices, they did not have to live with the major consequences that affect so many living for fun with no attachment to holiness. Pregnancies, addictions and diseases are just a sampling of the things that some students carry around because they think that it is all right to disregard God's standards and do what seems fun at the time. Even worse, these youth leave their influence on other students, who face their own consequences when they allow themselves to be led astray.

God does have standards, and he does expect believers to do whatever is possible to align their lives with them. He realizes that we will not be perfect while we are on this planet, but to ignore holiness and rationalize wrongdoing is dangerous. Every time we neglect God's standards, we are moving away from holiness. The habits our students build into their young lives will many times continue into adulthood.

We must long to see our students embrace God in a way that will help them make purity a priority. They must understand that God asks them to be holy because he is holy (see 1 Peter 1:16).

BRINGING IT BACK

When apathy has infected students to the point that they ignore God's conviction, they must be held accountable for their choices and encouraged to make better ones. Here are some suggestions that will assist you as you strive to make a difference with young people who do not value holiness and purity.

Pray. Because these students tend to stubbornly cling to their beliefs and practices, we must invoke the help of the Almighty. We will surely lose this battle if we fight it without him, but with his assistance we can win. We need to focus our prayer on inward matters and not just on the students' actions. For example, we should pray that God will meet their need for companionship, not just that he will protect them from wrong relationships. We can ask him to give them a passion for righteousness so that they might have a holy boldness in the face of temptation.

We can also aggressively pray Philippians 1:9-11: "And this is my prayer for Denise: Lord, let your love abound to her more and more in knowledge and depth of insight, so that she may be able to discern what is best and that she may be pure and blameless until the day of Christ, filled with the fruit of righteousness that comes through Jesus Christ—to the glory and praise of God."

A prayer of confession is simple yet significant. Their slates are cleaned; they can begin to walk toward holiness.

Recognize that repentance is needed. If there is sin, repentance is needed. There is no way around it. Recognizing this will give you a clear direction as you pray, prepare and work with your students. Communicate to them that repentance is more than a simple act of speaking words. Explain that it is a spiritual action that results in forgiveness (see 1 John 1:9).

True repentance moves students away from the immorality and sin that have littered their past and toward a new commitment to holiness. This type of repentance establishes strong convictions while removing previous mistakes.

Be bold yet loving. When you talk about holiness with your students, you are communicating God's message to them, and for that reason you can be bold. Some people think that they can't be bold and loving at the same time, but that is not the case. God's standards are high, but he offers as much grace and mercy as we need. Be strong in your message, but don't neglect the aspect of forgiveness. Communicate God's expectations for your students, but also share his love with them. By doing so you will give them hope that they can be acceptable in God's eyes.

Don't talk about the rules; present holiness as a cause. Teenagers struggle to respond to rules, but they will embrace a cause. When they think you are trying to make them conform to your laws, they will ignore you. Most of them, however, want to believe that God has a plan for them, and if you can persuade them that holiness is a just cause, one that benefits them (the story of King Saul in 1 Samuel 13-15 is a good example of the consequences of ignoring holiness), then they will see a reason to pursue it.

A NEW GENERATION

God expects integrity and purity. While he knows we're not perfect, he expects us to do our best to live up to his standards. Although we must be careful not to get wrapped up in legalism, we cannot continue to ignore the sins that are saturating the lives of our students. We cannot let them continue to believe that their lives can be lived separately from their faith. We cannot allow them to continue showing others a poor representation of God's character. With God's Word in our hands and mouths and his Spirit going before us, we must begin to raise up a generation that values holiness.

11

HEALING AND HOPE
ARE ON THE WAY

Samantha seemed to have everything under control. She always had a calm demeanor, managing to smile and laugh even after a big fight with her parents. When her boyfriend forced himself on her and then ended the relationship, she played it off like it was no big deal. Her grades fell, but she had ready excuses. Her ability to say all the right things kept everyone around her unaware of the real problems that were boiling deep down in her heart.

One Saturday afternoon, all the pain Samantha had been storing away for years finally came out for everyone to see. In the stillness of her empty home, her insecurities clamored and her feelings of hopelessness reached the boiling point. She raided every medicine cabinet in the house and quickly consumed about eighty-five pills. Her parents arrived home to discover their daughter passed out on the couch.

An ambulance ride and a stomach pump later, Samantha was conscious again, and now the physical pain that she felt seemed to illustrate the emotional pain she had been hoarding. But at least now everyone knew what was going on inside her.

Samantha's Christianity had been nothing more than a social outlet; she had never known what to do with all of the baggage that life handed her. She had never been taught that God was waiting to sit and connect with her. If she had known the comfort and encouragement she could find in his presence, she might not have fallen as far as she did.

GENERATION OF PAIN

Shallow, apathetic Christianity is sometimes more destructive and isolating than not having any connection to God at all. People who have mediocre relationships with God do not think of him as a friend or counselor and so do not run to him with their hurts. Like Samantha, they bottle up their true feelings until they reach a point where the pain they have given refuge to sneaks up on them and explodes, surprising them as well as those around them.

Those who come close to God discover a friend and counselor in their times of need.

Everything in Joey's life was translated through his impression that he was an oddball and that no one really liked him or cared what happened to him. His wounds, though not always visible, were always present, affecting his relationships and stealing his confidence.

His moodiness was frustrating to those around him, but it didn't irritate anyone nearly as much as it did him, because he had no control over it. Without warning, he could slip into an emotional funk and remain there for days or even weeks on end. He had problems sleeping, and his eating habits were sporadic, causing his weight and energy level to fluctuate daily. He was convinced that he didn't look right, wasn't bright enough and was a social misfit. He tried to hide his insecurities, which only served to reinforce the feelings he was trying to escape from. Because depression, guilt and pain had been at the forefront of his life for so long, he had lost hope for a positive future and had pondered suicide.

Many of the people in Joey's life authentically cared for him, but he could not accept it. He had problems trusting anyone because the people who should have been trustworthy in his past had proven themselves to be manipulative, abusive and unfaithful. His lack of trust even affected his relationship with God. Whenever he heard someone say that God loved him, Joey would just roll his eyes.

Joey's need was occasionally so strong that it would send him into a lonely place where he would beg God for an encouraging word and yet still lapse into sorrow. He was unable to hear God's kind whispers because of the amplified emotions in his heart. He longed for happiness but felt handcuffed to a life of torment and pain. Because he never learned to embrace Christ's ability to heal wounds and overcome insecurities, he continues to struggle with hope, joy and faith.

The devil has worked hard to destroy our students through painful circumstances. He works to convince them that they are not valuable and that they have no hope of anything better. When they believe this, they become easy to manipulate. They won't protect what they don't consider to be precious. If they don't know their true identity in Christ, and if they don't know God as a loving Father, they will seek love in the wrong places, value in things that are meaningless and comfort in places that are temporary.

In the past couple of years, I have heard our students referred to as the "generation of pain" because they have known more abandonment and abuse than any generation has before them. The young people in our world today need healing and hope. They have been left feeling wounded and alone for too long. It is time that they are introduced to the One who can bring comfort and peace when there is none to be found.

HEALING AND HOPE

God knew that some of us would struggle to see a time in the future when we would be free from the painful memories of the past. That is why he promised that there will be a day when "you will forget the shame of your youth" (Isaiah 54:4). As people who love and teach students, it is our responsibility to help them reach that goal sooner rather than later.

Pray. We must pray that God will protect our young people from the negative memories and troubling circumstances that so many of them face. We can also pray that they will make wise decisions and that negative relationships will not draw them away from righteous and pure living. However, when dealing with students who have already been attacked or who are already dealing with wounds, we need to do more than just pray from a defensive posture. We must pray aggressively against both the memories and the effects of the pain our students are experiencing.

Make the Bible the source. Our students need to embrace biblical truth regarding their identity in Christ and their value in his eyes if they are to successfully face their hurts and find comfort from their troubles. As adults we play key roles in helping that happen. By continually reminding our students of what God says about them and by doing our best to exhibit unconditional love, we can reinforce the knowledge that God loves them and cares about them.

Repeat yourself. Daily the media, society and the devil work to convince young people that their crises are here to stay and that their emotions are justified. In order for students to learn otherwise, the positive voices in their life must be just as tenacious. Don't think that saying it once will be enough. Chances are they will fall back into their old patterns and need to be reminded again that there is hope. Don't give up and don't be afraid to sound redundant. They may seem tired of hearing the same thing from you over and over again, but they will recall what you said when they need it most.

I am persistent in speaking my love to my daughters. They might roll their eyes and say, "I know," but I pray that when they hear the

lies of "No one cares about you," the constant reminder of my love
will carry them through.

Encourage and comfort. One day while doing my personal devotions I stumbled upon a verse that challenged the way I was relating
to teenagers: "For you know that we dealt with each of you as a father
deals with his own children, encouraging, comforting and urging you
to live lives worthy of God, who calls you into his kingdom and glory"
(1 Thessalonians 2:11-12). I realized that I was spending all of my
time urging my students to live righteous lives and be faithful witnesses to others, but I wasn't taking any time to encourage them and
comfort them. God began to show me that if I wanted my students to
respond to my challenges, I needed to offer them those things as well.

I know a parent who figured this out midstream, and it made all
the difference in the world. When her son was fourteen, he was doing
poorly in school, choosing friends she didn't approve of and lying to
her. Assuming he was being rebellious, this mother began to talk
with her son daily about the difference between right and wrong. Although the things she was saying were true, her son didn't respond,
because all he heard was his mother preaching at him.

Then one day the mother realized that her son was not rebellious
but frustrated. He was actually angry with himself for not having the
courage to stand up to his friends. He was mad that he wasn't living
out his convictions or talking about his faith. She realized that she
needed to stop lecturing her son concerning his behavior and start
encouraging him in his ability to be strong. Instead of praying that he
would stop lying, she began to pray that he would develop stronger
convictions and a boldness to stand up for what he knew was right.
She began to say "I love you" more often, and she began to remind
him that despite all of his failures, God still loved him and had a great
plan for his life.

After a few weeks she saw a visible difference in her son. His spiritual life became more of a priority, his relationship with his mom became more open, and his confidence began to grow. The things that had made his mom think he was rebellious began to fall away as God gave him a stronger desire for holiness.

NO MORE PAIN

The "generation of pain" needs to know that God is waiting to love them, whatever their circumstances. They need to know that they are not alone, that they never have been and never will be. It is our job to help convince them of that awesome fact. Apathy thrives on pity and pain, but its effects are destroyed in the awesome presence of a loving God.

12   INSTILLING SECURITY

Mandy was beautiful, athletic and popular, but she didn't realize it. As she was growing up, her father had wounded her with sarcastic comments. She thought she was stupid and fat, and she assumed that was what everyone else saw when they looked at her. It affected the way she felt about herself and how she approached relationships. One day she said to me, "I have heard you say that God loves me and thinks I am perfect, but I don't feel that way."

Sincerely, I looked her in the eyes and declared, "Mandy, I could sit here all day and try to convince you that God does love you and that you are perfect, but you aren't even able to hear my words. And that is okay. But you do need to hear God. Every day, he tries to whisper in your ear and tell you that he loves you. Every minute, God is trying to get your attention so that you can see the smile on his face when he is thinking about you." A tear formed on her cheek. "Mandy," I continued, "I think the world of you, but more important, God gave the world for you . . . because he thought you were worth it!"

I wanted so badly for Mandy to know how precious she was, but I knew that I couldn't convince her of that. Only when Mandy began to spend time with God and let him embrace her with his love would she find true peace and self-confidence.

CAN YOU SEE WHAT THEY SEE?

One of the direct results of apathy in students' lives is an inability to stay focused on what God says about who they are, what they can become and what they can do. This allows room for the lies that saturate their perceptions and tell them that they must meet certain standards and have the approval of others to have value.

The attack is strong, but our God is stronger. Even though the mirror may shout lies about their own frailties, God can help our students to overcome them. One of the first steps in doing so is recognizing where the wrong images are coming from. The attack is on many fronts, but a few of the most aggressive and damaging are listed here.

False images in the media. The chiseled bodies, perfect faces and smooth voices that Hollywood promotes have done damage to the confidence of many people of all ages. These standards have been adopted as not only desirable but necessary for success, popularity and happiness. As the media applauds the beautiful and ignores the average, students struggle to find significance when they realize that they don't measure up to those standards.

Wounding words that stick. Even if they aren't intended to wound, negative words can paralyze their victims. Words that seem harmless can plant themselves in a person's memory and, watered and fertilized by insecurities, can develop into overwhelming and debilitating wounds.

I once knew a man who grew up with a distorted image of himself because of the words of an uncle he looked up to. Although this man loved his nephew, for the sake of humor he would poke fun at him. Because the boy worked so hard to hide the pain, it looked as if he was ignoring the remarks altogether. However, he had begun to believe that he was "funny looking" and "dumb." He stopped trying in school and eventually ended up dropping out. Because one of his heroes spoke negative words about him, the course of his life was dramatically affected.

Comparisons. When what students see in the mirror is clouded because they are continually comparing themselves with others, their self-esteem will suffer and they will search for their identity in wrong places.

I once met a student who did not like what she saw in the mirror because it didn't measure up with what she saw living in the room next to her. Although she was popular, she wasn't as popular as her older sister had been when she was in high school. Even though she was funny, she couldn't entertain the entire crowd like her sister had. As athletic as she was, she couldn't match her sister's accomplishments. Trying to gain ground, she worked to get more attention and gain more respect, but the harder she tried, the more she found herself trapped in her sister's shadow.

Past failures. When I was a teen, my inability to live out my promises to God haunted me. Although no one knew about my insecurities, I had already decided that I was a failure. When I looked in the mirror, I did not see who I was; I saw who I had been, and it stole my ability to believe that I could be anything better. When students cannot forget the failures of the past, they are unable to build a strong future. As long as their history is at the center of their memories, their potential will be untapped.

Seclusion. People are different socially. Some are introverts, others are extroverts. Certain types of people are continually surrounded by crowds, while others can walk through the world without interrupting anyone else's life. Sometimes the tendencies are built because of personal preference, but other times the dynamics are difficult to pinpoint.

Even if students are isolated by choice, they can still struggle to understand why there are no people around them. They can still feel like no one likes them. Isolation can cause self-doubt, which leads to low self-esteem.

CHANGING THEIR PERCEPTIONS

As we read through the Bible we can see that everything that God does is intentional. Nothing is random or a fluke. When he walked in the garden with Adam and Eve, he knew that he was investing in them. When he called Abraham to be the father of his nation, he did not let Abraham carve out his journey alone. As David grew and developed into a great leader and a man after God's heart (see Acts 13:22), God was with him, and each bit of his life was built specifically for the future. In the same way, Jesus did not just call the twelve disciples because he wanted an entourage. Rather, he wanted to train them, to teach them through his words and his life.

As God chose people and invested in them, one of his goals was to help them see themselves through his eyes. He helped them see past their insecurities and limitations and realize that they had been fashioned for a purpose. They had God on their side and weren't lacking anything that was needed for achieving success. God knew that if these people were isolated from him and had only other people in their life, they would not have the confidence to be effective. However, if they spent time with him, their perspectives would change and their trust in what God had done in them and could do through them would grow exponentially.

Everything that God does is intentional. Nothing is random or a fluke.

The same goes for our students. If their only influences are coming from society, then their insecurities will rage and their weaknesses will be glaring. If that happens, they will be paralyzed instead of mobilized. However, if they spend time with Christ, they will be affected by his views of them and injected with confidence.

The time that our students spend investing in their spiritual life will drastically impact their self-esteem. However, we have the opportunity to communicate their importance and assure them that they are loved.

When it comes to convincing students of their value, it is not your communication skills that will be your greatest tool. The greatest asset you have is your time. Instead of rushing through these important relationships, take the time to listen to your students' words and discover the condition of their heart. Time shows value, and if you value students enough to spend time with them, they will begin to realize that they truly are important. By listening to them, you will convince them that you believe in them, and that belief will inspire them to believe in themselves.

Encourage positive talk. One of the ways insecure people both reveal themselves and reinforce their lack of confidence is through the self-defacing comments that they make. If you want to move your students from unhealthy self-perceptions to ones that are strong and based on biblical truths, you must help them overcome their own comments. Have a conversation with them about the negative things they say about themselves. Only when the unhealthy remarks stop will they be able to move toward a healthy self-image.

Avoid teasing. It is imperative that you don't contribute to students' poor self-esteem with your words, even if you mean no harm by them. I have learned from personal experience that students often embrace flippant comments as truth, even if the remarks were made jokingly. The negative things you say will stay with them much longer than the positive ones.

You are responsible for the wounds you cause, whether they are intentional or not.

Point them to the Word. When

working with students who are paralyzed by the images that they see in the mirror, one of the most effective things you can do is to get them to recognize and embrace what God's Word says about them. One good way to do that is to teach students to personalize the Scriptures. For example, you can teach them to pray Psalm 139 as follows: "Lord, I thank you that you created my inmost being. You knit me together in my mother's womb. I praise you because I am fearfully and wonderfully made; your works are wonderful, I know that full well. My frame was not hidden from you when I was made in the secret place. When I was woven together in the depths of the earth, your eyes saw my unformed body." Other effective Scriptures are Zephaniah 3:17, Zechariah 2:8-9, 2 Corinthians 5:21 and Ephesians 2:10. When students who are struggling with their self-worth begin to pray these powerful words audibly, the truth will eventually sink into their heart and transform their perceptions.

Early in her twenties Megan came to our discipleship school as a servant-hearted, godly woman with suffering self-esteem. She knew her emotions were deceiving her, but she still felt awkward, ignorant, clumsy and unattractive. During her time with us, however, her perceptions started to change as she sought God in his Word. I can remember times when I would walk past the prayer room at our ministry and hear her reciting the Scriptures or praying through the Psalms. Confidence began to replace her timidity, and she began to come out of her shell and volunteer for projects that she originally had avoided.

Today Megan is attending a Christian college where she is an aggressive and impressive leader, not because she is socially outgoing but because she is spiritually strong. During the summers she works in intense inner-city situations that would have scared her just a few years ago. Because she began to pursue God's heart for her, her beliefs about herself changed. She is a living reminder to me that anyone's self-perception can improve if they take the time to get close to God's presence and let his Word do its work.

BRINGING TRUTH INTO THEIR PERSPECTIVES

Whether they feel fat, ugly or stupid, you can't tell them anything different. Their perception is stronger than your reality. How they came to feel this way isn't as important as the fact that they do feel this way. What they see when they look in the mirror will determine how they live their life, how they relate to God and how effective they will be in fulfilling their God-given purpose. For these reasons, we must work to see their perceptions change.

Ben was obsessed with his dream of becoming a famous musician. He spent hours practicing and writing music. He worked on his stage persona and his wardrobe, practiced signing autographs, and considered how he would present himself in interviews. He studied the musicians he respected and was a walking encyclopedia of music history. Music was his means of relaxation, his escape when he felt moody and the main thing by which he chose and related to his friends. He was definitely focused.

Ben was so consumed with music that he forgot all about God. He still went to church with his parents, but when he was there he evaluated the worship service and thought about how he would do it differently. His Bible sat on a shelf, he never prayed, and he avoided spiritual conversations with those around him. Although he was not involved in anything immoral, he was so focused on one element of his life that he never took time to invest in his relationship with God.

Years have passed since I was Ben's youth pastor, and now he is an adult. The music industry teased him for a season, but he never found the success that he wanted. He is frustrated and discouraged, and in the midst of all of his disillusionment he still has not realized that God is daily trying to get through to him.

ARE THEIR PASSIONS WRONG?

As human beings created in the image of a passionate God, it is impossible for our students not to be passionate as well. We all were created with different desires, purposes and goals, and when used wisely they are what will make us successful at our God-intended life's work. However, when those passions begin to overshadow our passion for the One who gave us those desires, something is wrong.

I am not suggesting that we must strip our students of everything in their lives that is not a spiritual pursuit. The passions in and of themselves are not wrong. Our goal is not to make our students conform to our ideas of what God wants them to be. Instead, we must work to help them keep their eyes focused on their relationship with their Lord first and foremost. We must teach them to evaluate their priorities honestly while at the same time giving them permission to be who God made them to be.

The question is not "Are they passionate?" but "What are they passionate about?"

DISCOVERING THEIR OBSESSIONS

The first step in helping our students use their passions as God has intended is recognizing the distractions that have stolen their attention. We pursue the things that are important to us, so if you want to know what students have prioritized in their life, take an inventory of what they spend their time on. Attentively listen for the things that dominate their conversations. Although it would be great if our students talked about God when they were interacting with their peers, most teenagers spend all of their time talking about sports, relationships, entertainment or other things that are shallow but captivating in their lives.

When students have a goal or an obsession, they often want to be defined by it. They believe their obsessions are what makes them valuable, and they throw all of their time into developing these things, fearing the day when they may lose them.

Several years ago at a barbecue my attention fell on six young men who all had one thing in common: they were all drummers. As I listened to their conversation, I realized that the only thing that they knew to talk about was music. They were either discussing equipment and different gigs that they had played at, or they were talking about bands.

Walking over to their table, I threw out a challenge. I asked them if they could go for five minutes without talking about music in any way. A couple of them looked concerned, but two or three spurred everyone on to take my challenge. The moment that the five minutes began, they all fell into an uncomfortable silence. After about thirty seconds someone broke in with a forced, "So, how about them Broncos?" Everyone laughed and then went silent again.

They did make it the entire five minutes without talking about music. Actually, they went the entire five minutes without talking about anything. These normally talkative young men did not know what to discuss if they couldn't talk about their obsession.

Students' conversations will reveal their passions. Once we've discovered their passions, we must encourage them to consider the priority they place on them. Are they allowing their passions to push God out of the picture?

REFOCUSING

God's earnest desire is for every Christian to have a deep and intimate relationship with him. He wants every one of our students to be consumed with him, to make him the top priority. Yet all too often, students give the majority of their affections to something other than God. They may actually be pursuing their God-given talents and passions, but they leave God out of the process.

Say, for example, that a young woman has great talent as an athlete. It would be easy for her to move athletics to the top spot in her life and neglect the God who gave her that talent. Does God want her to succeed? Of course. But is he satisfied to be put on the back burner while she pursues her dream? Absolutely not. It is imperative that we get our students to understand that while God did create them with gifts and passions, designing them for a specific plan and purpose (see Jeremiah 29:11; Ephesians 2:10), his first concern is that they have a healthy connection with him. Through that connection they will be able to use the passions he has given them and pursue the plans he has laid out for them.

If we are going to see our students refocus their attention on Christ, we must begin by praying that God will make them uncomfortable in their apathy and distraction. Then we need to pray that their focus will be redirected toward Christ alone. We can use Colossians 3:1-4 as a personal prayer for our students: "Since she has been raised with Christ, help her to set her heart on things above where Christ is seated at the right hand of God. Set her mind on things above, not on earthly things. For her life is hidden with Christ in God."

HUMILITY BREEDS GREATNESS

First Peter 5:5-6 says,

> "God opposes the proud
>   but gives grace to the humble."
> Humble yourselves, therefore, under God's mighty hand, that
> he may lift you up in due time.

Have you ever seen a father wrestle with his little boy and put his hand on his son's forehead to hold him back? Try as he might, the little boy can't reach his dad, but that doesn't steal his energy. He keeps trying, thinking that at any time he will break past his dad's defenses. Without God in the proper place in our priorities, we will find an invisible hand planted on our forehead preventing us from making progress—even if our goal is God-inspired.

On the other hand there is the picture of the little boy whose father doesn't hold him back but rather opens doors for him. With a guiding hand the father leads his son through doorways where possibilities await. When we are humble and submitted to God, he will lead us into new opportunities where our passions can be explored and used as they were intended.

One of the fun things about speaking at music festivals is that I get to spend some time backstage with the musicians. I have discovered that some of the most authentic people in the music industry today are also the ones who are the most popular. Although they may deal with pride in their own ways, they have humbled themselves enough that God has been able to use their talents to reach great numbers of people for the kingdom.

On the other hand, I have noticed that some of the lesser known, struggling bands are so prideful that they make a person feel like he's inconveniencing them if he even says hello to them. The more popular musicians are not necessarily any more talented than these struggling bands, but their attitudes are different. God has exalted the humble and opposed the proud. Our students must realize that their motives are more important to God than their talents. We must encourage them to walk in humility if we desire to see their passions develop to their fullest potential.

OPENING DOORS

One of the most difficult battles for us as humans is finding the balance between confidence and cockiness. Students who struggle with
misplaced priorities need constant reminders that instead of focusing
on selfish ambition, they must embrace humility and service. You can
help them by offering to hold them accountable. Ask them simple
questions like, "Are you taking the credit for something God did
through you?" Commit to pray for and with them about this issue.
With their priorities in place and God at the top, they will see doors
to exciting opportunities opening before them.

14

WHY DO THEY GRADUATE FROM THEIR FAITH?

It seemed like just yesterday that his relationship with God had been intact and thriving. When he realized that he was living for himself in a world of regrets and broken promises, he humbled his heart before God and asked for forgiveness. Instantly, it was granted. But there was still work to be done. He had to figure out how he had ever fallen so far away so that he could make sure it never happened again.

In high school he had been doing great. *What changed?* he asked himself. *What made my relationship with God back then so stable?* He thought about how his parents had always been right there to remind him to stay faithful to his devotions and about how the leaders of the youth group he had attended had been a positive influence on him. He realized that he had always had other Christians in his life to encourage him to build his faith. Now, away at college, he no longer had those influences and did not know how to connect with God on his own. He felt alone and discouraged as he tried to figure out how to get back to where he had been.

WE CAN T LET THEM GRADUATE FROM THEIR FAITH

When students graduate from high school and move away from home, many of them also graduate from their faith. An immeasurable number of young Christians are quietly living their faith only in the context of those around them—friends, youth pastors and parents who encourage them in their spiritual journeys. These students do not know how to be alone with God because they constantly have other people in their life to give them advice, direction and affirmation. Although they seem energized in the presence of companions, they are spiritually apathetic when the room is empty. This problem may hide itself for a season, but when the students' circumstances change (they leave home or a spiritual leader moves away) the spiritual disaster will present itself.

Here are a few of the characteristics that tend to define those who live their faith only in the context of companionship.

Instability. Students who live their faith only at the urging of others tend to live on a roller coaster. When they attend youth services, camps, conferences or special events, they visit the mountaintop for a time, but they are never able to sustain that intimacy with God. They bottom out as soon as the "feeling" is gone because when they are alone they neglect their relationship with God.

Faithlessness. These students see spiritual groups as a benefit but not a necessity. Therefore, if problems arise or if their social needs are not being met, they leave the group, using any excuse they can find to rationalize their behavior. I learned this as a teenager. One of my peers at church decided one day that he was unappreciated. He confessed at a restaurant that he was not going to come back to church until five people called him and told him that they missed him. Because he only connected with God through our group, when he did leave (and he never came back), he walked away not only from our church but also from God.

Follower tendencies. Because these students prioritize relationships over their faith, they tend to be followers who are easily swayed by the opinions of those around them. That is why, when they no longer have companions to offer direction, they feel helpless and confused.

Lack of focus. Because they are continually searching to strengthen friendships and reinforce their social position, they struggle to focus on the important things. During prayer, they talk. In the middle of services, they mess around. While on work projects and missions trips, these students value conversation over service.

Strong social relationships (no matter how spiritual) cannot replace the love relationship with Christ that is the foundation for spiritual growth and health. Horizontal relationships may change, but the vertical relationship we build with Christ will always be available to us.

CREATING A CONSISTENT LEARNING CURVE

If our students enroll in a growing relationship with God, they will never want to graduate. Students who don't yet know how to grow on their own need strong leaders who can help them stay focused and teach them to discover authentic faith and intimate connection with God. To keep our students growing and building their faith apart from their spiritual support systems, we must consistently encourage them to connect with God.

Don't wait for a formal conversation to try to influence them; use your casual times together as well. Let them catch you reading your Bible, memorizing Scripture or in an intimate moment with God. If the opportunity arises, actually invite them to participate in a one-on-one study session

If our students enroll in a growing relationship with God, they'll never want to graduate from it.

with you. As they see you living out intimacy with God, they will find this relationship practical and exciting in their own life as well.

When Eastman and Angel arrived at my church when I was a teenager, they instantly became my heroes. What caught my attention were their personalities: young, fun and crazy. As I got to know them, however, it was their authentic faith and passionate zeal for God that held my attention. Eastman shared with me how he had struggled with and overcame his weaknesses, and Angel modeled her devotional life, shared her convictions on dating and displayed a genuine love for God. As I spent substantial time with my new youth pastors, I wanted to be like them in the way that they approached God, lived their lives and impacted the world. Their hunger inspired me, the love they had for Christ captivated me, and their quest to know God challenged me. The influence they had on me continues to affect my spiritual life today, and this is the same kind of impact we can have on our students as we share with them our life and personal pursuit of God.

Help them build a strong devotional life. Your students may want to develop a healthy devotional life and simply do not know how. By recommending (and providing them with) good devotional materials, you can help them begin to build this habit. Make sure that you are available to answer questions but also to teach them to research the answers for themselves and ask God for his revelation.

Affirm them. Go out of your way to notice and affirm your students if you know that they are meeting with God. Tell them that you see a difference in their life as a result and that you are proud of them. Even if their motives are not pure right away (perhaps they are putting in devotional time simply to receive affirmation from you), the time spent in connection to God will still have an influence on them.

Establish accountability. Find ways of building accountability into your students' devotional lives, both between you and them and between them and their peers. Many students simply forget that they are supposed to spend time with God. Their lives are filled with things that distract them and they end up neglecting the things that are most important. By holding them accountable, you aren't putting pressure on them; you are simply helping them follow through on their convictions.

My sister-in-law had a friend who held her accountable in such a way. Every weekday morning, they would talk on the phone and ask each other, "Did you spend time with God yesterday? Is he asking you to do anything in regard to what he taught you?" I can't answer for Debbie, but I can tell you that if I knew I was getting a phone call and that I was going to have to answer those questions, I would not easily forget that I needed to get with God. Such accountability may add fuel to your students' fire.

SENDING THEM OFF ON THEIR OWN

Strong families, youth ministries and Christian friends are wonderful things for students to have in their life. But if we allow our students to depend on these companions to hold them up in their faith, we are setting them up for failure.

As Jesus was preparing to leave his disciples and return to heaven, he knew it was important for them to learn to walk with God on their own. He did not want them to move away from God because he was no longer there to guide them. In John 17 we find a prayer that he prayed for them as they were getting ready to graduate into a new season of their lives:

> I have revealed you to those whom you gave me out of the world. They were yours; you gave them to me and they have obeyed your word. . . . I pray for them. I am not praying for the world, but for those you have given me, for they are yours. . . . Holy Father, protect them by the power of your name. . . . My prayer is not that you take them out of the world but that you protect them from the evil one. . . . Sanctify them by the truth. (John 17:6-17)

Amen!

CONCLUSION

BUILDING IN DESIRE

One Sunday while standing in an airport waiting to catch a plane, I locked eyes with a seven-year-old girl in a wheelchair. I smiled at her and waved, and she waved back. I watched her from a distance, and even though I didn't get close enough to talk to her, I recognized in her a gentle spirit that was both sweet and entrancing. Then, right before the plane began to board, her happy countenance turned into one of tragic crisis.

Because she had already won my heart, I wanted to know what had upset her. I eavesdropped on the conversation that her mother was having with a grandmotherly woman next to her and learned that the reason for the outburst was that the girl had just realized that she was going to miss Sunday school. This beautiful little girl who had been smiling all morning had become inconsolable at the thought of missing church.

WOULDN'T IT BE NICE?

Wouldn't it be nice if our students (and we, for that matter) were as addicted to meeting with God as that little girl was to getting to her church? Wouldn't it be nice if the young people we care about and labor for were so captivated by Christ and so sold on the prospect of spending time in his presence that if they went through a day without their time alone with him they would be upset?

When people truly hunger after God, they have to be near him. They don't want to miss one day, and they aren't satisfied unless they sense his presence and hear his voice. I am convinced that these are the people who will so completely surrender to God that they will themselves be changed and become the ones who revolutionize the world. What is more, I am certain that we could see an entire generation of students turn into this type of Christian.

OUR MANDATE

A generation is in the balance. Apathy is their enemy, and spiritual hunger is their ally. We are called to combat the apathy that will both lead to our students' destruction and prevent them from making a difference in the world. As parents and leaders, we cannot be satisfied with students who are self-obsessed and uninterested in spiritual things. We must help them overcome their complacency and understand that a vital and relevant relationship with their Creator is not only appealing but very attainable.

How will our students be remembered? Will they be known only as good church kids with strong morals who regularly attended church and wore Christian T-shirts? Or will they be remembered as the generation that brought passion back to the church as they learned to live in God's presence? "Lord Jesus, may our young people long to be near you. May they know your voice and be addicted to your presence. God, drive off apathy and ignite their hearts with passion for you. May they be the generation that seeks your face and surrenders to your will. Show us how to lead them directly to you; after all, they are yours to begin with. Amen."

FURTHER READING

Augsburger, David. *Caring Enough to Confront*. Revised edition. Glendale, Calif.: Regal, 1980.

Barna, George. *Real Teens: A Contemporary Snapshot of Youth Culture*. Glendale, Calif.: Regal, 2001. Online at <www.kff.org/entmedia/3229-index.cfm>.

Everts, Don. *Jesus with Dirty Feet*. Downers Grove, Ill.: InterVarsity Press, 1999.

————. *The Smell of Sin and the Fresh Air of Grace*. Downers Grove, Ill.: InterVarsity Press, 2003.

Higgs, Mike. *Youth Ministry from the Inside Out: How Who You Are Shapes What You Do*. Downers Grove, Ill.: InterVarsity Press, 2003.

Smith, Efrem. *Raising Up Young Heroes*. Downers Grove, Ill.: InterVarsity Press, 2004.

Tokunaga, Paul, et al. *Faith on the Edge: Daring to Follow Jesus*. Downers Grove, Ill.: InterVarsity Press, 1999.

Wakabayashi, Allen Mitsuo. *Kingdom Come: How Jesus Wants to Change the World*. Downers Grove, Ill.: InterVarsity Press, 2003.

Sean Dunn is the founder and president of Champion Ministries, whose mission is to creatively and effectively communicate God's Word, his love and his purpose to every student between the ages of twelve and twenty-four. For a free newsletter and list of materials from Champion Ministries, or for information on having Sean Dunn minister at your church, conference, retreat, school or other ministry group, please contact the ministry at

Champion Ministries
P.O. Box 1323
Castle Rock, CO 80104
Phone: 303-660-3582
E-mail: champion@championministries.org